RICHARD CON

THE
CATHOLIC FAITH

A DOMINICAN'S VISION

GEOFFREY
CHAPMAN

Geoffrey Chapman
A Cassell imprint
Villiers House, 41/47 Strand, London WC2N 5JE
387 Park Avenue South, New York, NY 10016–8810

First published 1994

British Library Cataloguing-in-Publication Data
A catalogue record for this book is available from the British Library.

Library of Congress Cataloging-in-Publication Data
Applied for.

ISBN 0–225–66685–5

In accordance with Canon 832 approval is given for the publication of this
book.
Nihil obstat: Columba Ryan OP and Aidan Nichols OP (censors)
Imprimi potest: Malcolm McMahon OP, Prior Provincial
25 March 1994

In accordance with Canon 827.3 approval is given for the publication
of this book.
Nihil obstat: Philip J. Kerr STL, Censor Deputatus
Imprimatur: ✠ Keith Patrick O'Brien, Archbishop of St Andrews and
Edinburgh
8 February 1994

Unless otherwise noted, Scripture quotations are from the Revised Standard
Version, Catholic edition (Nelson, 1966).

Quotations from the *Catechism of the Catholic Church*, English translation for
United Kingdom and Ireland, copyright © 1994 Geoffrey Chapman–Libreria
Editrice Vaticana, are used by permission.

Cover pictures:
From the Hours of Our Lady (MS Can. Liturg., folio 108; 179 c 7), Flemish
manuscript from *c.* 1400, Bodleian Library, Oxford.
Photo: The Bodleian Library, Oxford

Andrei Rublev, *The Old Testament Trinity.*
Andrei Rublev Museum, Moscow. Photo: SVS Press

Back cover author photo: Newspix, Birmingham

Typeset by York House Typographic Ltd.
Printed and bound in Great Britain by
Biddles Ltd, Guildford and King's Lynn

CONTENTS

———— ❧ ————

FOREWORD

————— ❧ —————

THIS is an uncompromising but intelligent and attractive presentation of the traditional teaching of the Roman Catholic Church. Richard Conrad OP shows that this teaching is neither unreasonable nor inhumane. In recent centuries our culture has tended to assume a contradiction between reason and belief, between a love of the tradition and the spirit of inquiry. This book admirably challenges this opposition and invites us to discover the beauty and coherence of the doctrines of the Church. The author's scientific training – he has a doctorate in chemistry from Cambridge – is married to a deep theological grounding. This appears in many parts of the book, from exploration of how God's relationship to the world may be illustrated by the boiling of a kettle, to his discussion of whether we need believe that we are all descended from a single couple. This full-blooded presentation of the tradition is also marked by a deep sense of the mystery of God, and the limitations of all human language.

This book is clearly deeply influenced by Thomas Aquinas's *Summa Theologiae*, the most famous summary of Catholic teaching. It is structured by the great drama of our reception of all that we are from God, the giver of all good things and source of creation, and our return to God through redemption in Christ.

This God is, of course, the Trinitarian God. Conrad devotes an excellent chapter to introducing us to this central doctrine, so easily misunderstood, and so in need of clarification at a time when dialogue with our cousins of Judaism and Islam must be a central concern. He adopts Thomas's daring view that our relationship with this God is that of friendship, a sharing in the friendship that is the very life of God. Thus we are introduced to the extraordinary vision of the dignity of our human destiny, sharing in the life of God through the Spirit, called to be his children. We are taken way beyond a narrow view of morality as obedience to laws, the submission of our wills to external rules, to the more traditional and yet deeply attractive idea that we grow holy in growing in virtue, moving towards the fulfilment of our deepest wants in the utterly desirable God. The cross is shown not to be a sign of the God who is angry with sinners but a revelation of forgiveness.

I strongly recommend this book to anyone, especially a teacher, who wishes to have a clear and concise view of the doctrines of the Church, sensitive to questions that they raise for us today.

Fr Timothy Radcliffe OP
Master of the Order of Preachers
Rome, 10 March 1994

INTRODUCTION

Is there a God? This question is debated as much today as it has been for many years, and brilliant scientists, among others, think it is an important question. Some people claim that there is no need for God. Our modern, scientific theories explain all that needs to be explained, they say, leaving God with no job to do. Others claim that since science has shown us how incredibly wonderful and beautiful the universe is, it has taught us how great the Creator must be.

Many people, particularly Christians, Jews and Muslims, believe that there is one God, who has made the whole universe, and holds it in being. Great thinkers have written very carefully about how the world depends on God. If we view that dependence correctly, we can see that no scientific theory can 'relieve God of His[1] job'. For science can tell us *what kind* of universe we live in. But the 'job' of the Creator is not to plug the gaps in our understanding; it is something much more fundamental. God makes the universe *to be*. Without His creative love there would not be any kind of universe at all; there would be nothing for science to investigate, and no one to engage in science.

Christians are not alone in holding that there is a God who made and sustains the universe. But that is just the beginning of our faith. We believe that God has shown us, what we could not discover by ourselves, that His purpose is to do no less than share His own life and happiness with us! This offer of a share in God's own life has been made through Jesus Christ. He was born among the Jewish people, in Bethlehem, 2,000 years ago. After teaching and gathering disciples He was executed outside Jerusalem by being nailed to a cross on the day we call Good

Friday (probably in one of the years AD 30 or 33); the following Sunday He rose from the dead to a new and transformed life.

Jesus spoke of God as His Father, and of Himself as the Son; and He promised that as a result of His death and rising to new life we would be able to 'receive the Holy Spirit'. Therefore we believe that the life of the one God, who sustains the whole universe, is mysteriously rich: it is lived by Father, Son and Holy Spirit, in perfect union with each other. That is the life we are called to share. The Holy Spirit draws us into the relationship between the Son and the Father.

The Christian Faith gives us a vision to live by. We see the world as made and loved by God; we see ourselves called to live as God's children, reflecting His love and care, and sharing Christ's sorrow and joy as we journey towards the Father. The purpose of this book is to set out the main elements of the Christian faith and Christian life, as taught and lived by the Roman Catholic Church, the largest of the denominations into which, sadly, Jesus' followers have been divided.

Coming to faith – Augustine's story

There are many stories of how people have come to hold the Catholic faith. One of the most famous is the story of St Augustine, who was born in North Africa in the year AD 354 and died as Bishop of Hippo in 430. After he became Bishop he wrote his *Confessions*, in which he tells how God brought him to be a Catholic Christian, in response to the prayers of his mother, St Monica.

Although Monica was a Christian, Augustine was not baptized as a baby.[2] From the age of sixteen, he tells us, he began to indulge in sexual sins, and in the occasional act of vandalism with his companions. Wanting to pursue wisdom, he tried reading the Bible, but was put off by its style.[3] He fell in with the sect called the Manichees, who pointed to difficulties in the Bible, and seemed at first sight to explain the evil in the world better than the Christians did. The heavy material stuff of this world (including our bodies) they saw as evil; from it, the lighter spiritual stuff trapped in our bodies had to be set free.

After teaching rhetoric in Africa, Augustine moved to Rome, then to Milan to teach. He was beginning to see problems with the ideas of the Manichees, and was impressed by the preaching

of St Ambrose, Bishop of Milan. This helped him make sense of
the Bible, and correct his past misunderstandings of some
Christian teachings. He read the works of some pagan thinkers,
followers of Plato, the great ancient Greek philosopher. These
helped him see that things can exist, like God and the human
soul, which are not made of any kind of matter. He came to see
that evil is not a kind of material stuff, but wrong choices made
of our free will. He came to love the Christian God and to enjoy
reading the Bible.

But Augustine was afraid he would not be able to renounce
sexual sins and undertake to obey the Christian moral code.
Then he heard of the life of self-denial lived by the Egyptian
monk St Anthony, and was struck by St Paul's moral teaching.
At last he felt free of all that held him back, and went to be
baptized by St Ambrose.

Augustine returned to North Africa, where he worked as a
monk, as a priest, and finally as a Bishop, preaching, and
writing many books in defence of the Catholic faith and in
explanation of the Bible. In his *Confessions* he declared to God
'You have made us for Yourself, and our hearts are restless till
they rest in You'. Later, in his book *On the Trinity*, he showed
how the human mind was made in the image of God who is
Father, Son and Holy Spirit, and so can only find fulfilment in
communion with the God recognized by Christians, to which
goal it must be led by Jesus Christ, the Son of God made man.

Coming to faith – our own stories

In St Augustine's story there are many themes that recur in
other people's stories of coming to faith: quite often, similar
difficulties to his are overcome by the same kinds of help that he
received.

For example, people are often disturbed by the evils and
suffering in the world, and while they seek for an explanation of
evil, as St Augustine did, they wonder how a good God can be in
charge. Likewise our families and friends can influence us
towards or against the Christian and Catholic faith. Just as St
Augustine was inspired by hearing about St Anthony, people
today can be impressed by Christian figures like Mother
Teresa. So many different ideas about the world and its
meaning are put forth in our own time, as in St Augustine's

time, that it can be difficult to tell which make the most sense. It can be difficult to find out exactly what the Catholic Church teaches and why, and nowadays there are debates among Christians about whether certain of our doctrines need to be abandoned or re-interpreted; so just as St Augustine was helped by St Ambrose to understand the faith, good preachers and teachers are of great value today. Again, the moral teachings of the Catholic Church are different from the standards of society at large, as in the early centuries of Christianity, and this can put some people off accepting the Catholic faith.

St Augustine thought carefully, with the help of non-Christian as well as of Christian thinkers, and his concern to pursue the truth should be ours also. He found the truth, however, in Jesus Christ, and saw that human wisdom by itself could not have guessed at the depth of God's love for us that would be shown in the death of Jesus on the Cross. And he found the truth about Jesus in the Bible, as the Catholic Church interpreted it. We too should read the Bible, remembering that it is not easy to interpret without help, for it speaks of God's ways, which are mysterious, and it does so by means of words and images that need to be carefully savoured.

St Augustine wrote about his conversion to show what was the most important factor: he was led by God, who watched over his life even when he was not aware of it, and who drew him to love Him. God's care for Augustine was shown when He inspired St Monica to pray for her son, and when He inspired Augustine himself to pray long before he finally came home to the Catholic Church. So, when people today come to faith, that is because God cares for each one of them with a similar love. He will be inspiring the saints, and many people on earth, to pray for them, and those people may well find themselves praying to God, asking for guidance as He leads them into a deeper understanding of His ways.

This book offers some ways of seeing the beauty and coherence of the Catholic faith, and some answers to some of the difficulties in the way of faith. We cannot expect, in this life, complete answers to all our puzzles: by faith, supported by reason, we can see certain truths; and we can see that no arguments manage to disprove what we believe. Only when we know God as He is shall we see everything in His light.

How do we learn about the Catholic faith? – the Bible, the creeds, the Church's worship, the Church's teaching authorities

No words can express the full meaning of what God has done, or the depths of the love He has shown us. For this reason, the Catholic Church has never possessed a written document that sets out the whole of her[4] faith in such a way that nothing else would ever need to be said. But what has been shown to us is kept alive among us in two important ways, so that faith can be nourished.

One way is the *Bible*, the sacred Scriptures God Himself has inspired. The first part of the Bible, the *Old Testament*, was composed among the Jewish people in the thousand or so years before Christ. It tells how God formed a people for Himself, taught them about His love and His concern for justice, and inspired them to look forward to the coming of a Saviour. This history of hope led up to the coming of that Saviour, Jesus, the Son of God, and made it possible to understand who Jesus is and what He does for us. The *New Testament* was composed by the earliest followers of Jesus. It includes, for example, letters written by St Paul. Most importantly, it includes the four gospels, four 'portraits' of Jesus, the word *gospel* meaning 'good news'. The gospels concentrate on Jesus' public ministry and on His suffering and death, and describe how He was seen by some of His followers after His Resurrection from the dead. The gospels in particular deserve to be read and re-read. While the Church draws on the whole Bible in her worship, she reads the gospels with special reverence; and out of the Old Testament she makes special use of the Psalms. This collection of beautiful hymns and prayers has long formed the largest part of the Church's daily round of prayer.

Because of the difficulty of interpreting the Bible, because various groups on the fringe of the early Church used parts of it in rather odd ways, and because of later arguments about what to believe over particular issues, the Catholic Church has from early times drawn up short summaries of her faith, called *creeds* (from the Latin word *credo*, 'I believe'). These express succinctly what we believe the Bible tells us in more rich and varied language. One of the most important is called 'The Apostles' Creed':

I believe in God, the Father almighty, Creator of heaven and earth. I believe in Jesus Christ, His only Son, our Lord. He was conceived by the power of the Holy Spirit, and born of the Virgin Mary. He suffered under Pontius Pilate, was crucified, died and was buried. He descended to the dead. On the third day He rose again. He ascended into heaven, and is seated at the right hand of the Father. He will come again to judge the living and the dead. I believe in the Holy Spirit; the holy Catholic Church; the communion of Saints; the forgiveness of sins; the resurrection of the body; and the life everlasting. Amen.[5]

The composing of the creeds to summarize the basic elements of our faith is one of the ways in which the Church's *tradition* manifests itself. The Scriptures were composed among God's people, within their living tradition, and it is within the tradition of that same people that they must be preserved, read and interpreted.

The other important way in which what God has shown us is kept alive among us is in the Church's worship, especially in the seven rituals called *sacraments*, chief of which are Baptism and Holy Communion. These are the most significant element of the Church's tradition, for they have been celebrated, at Christ's command, from the Church's beginning.[6] They show us in the form of symbols what Jesus did for us, how God is drawing us to Himself, and what we hope for from God. We believe that they are more than symbols: Jesus is at work in them so that through them we are drawn to God and made receptive to further gifts. Because of their nature, the sacraments are particularly apt to show us the richness of God's plan which cannot be fully put into words. They deepen the vision faith gives us, and help us live by it.

Besides reading the Bible and taking part in the Church's worship, we can find out what the Church believes by reading or listening to what her *teaching authorities* have said and are saying. Sometimes, perhaps because conflicting accounts of the Church's faith in some area were being given, the Pope or a Council of Bishops[7] has declared with special authority what the Church does or does not believe. *We do not hold that God reveals new truths in this way*; but He does guide the Church so that she faithfully preserves the truths shown us in Jesus Christ and handed down by His first disciples. What may have been implicit in the Bible or the Sacraments can be 'defined' by such a special exercise of the teaching authority, or in various other ways made more explicit in the course of the Church's history.

So, besides those occasions when the Church's faith is defined with special solemnity, Popes and bishops have set out various aspects of the Church's faith for the instruction of the faithful, for example by means of sermons or letters or catechisms and other summaries of the faith. And important Christian thinkers, notably those we call 'Fathers' or 'Doctors' of the Church, have set out the faith carefully, giving reasons for it, and countering objections to it. The work still continues of setting out the same faith that the Church has always held, in ways that show its coherence and beauty to the people of today. In each age men and women are called to be *theologians*, that is, to think carefully about what God has shown us and to help others to understand something of it. But all those who are concerned to hold the full Catholic faith and who love God have access to the gift of the Holy Spirit which we call *wisdom*. This helps the whole body of the faithful relish good expressions of God's plan, and reject distortions of it, so that we can also appeal to the 'consensus of the faithful' as evidence for what truths are preserved in the Church's faith.

The most recent authoritative account of the Catholic Faith is the *Catechism of the Catholic Church*, promulgated in October 1992. I have taken short passages from it to serve as headings for many of the sections of this book, in which I present some of the key elements of the Church's faith, life and moral wisdom. The *Catechism* sets them out in much greater breadth than this book can – especially as regards moral teaching – but with the succinctness appropriate to a catechism.

Within the unity-in-diversity of the Catholic Church there are different theological traditions, a variety of ways of prayer, and many complementary roles and ministries. My chief guide is the great thirteenth-century Dominican theologian, St Thomas Aquinas,[8] whose understanding of human nature, language and society still fascinates many thinkers today, and who combined a profound sense of the majesty of God with an awareness of the gentleness with which God, dwelling within us, fulfils the needs He has given us.

NOTES

1 In many other languages than English, words have a grammatical gender. So in Latin, 'Trinity' is feminine and 'Word' – a title for the Son of God – is neuter. 'Spirit' is masculine in Latin, neuter in Greek and feminine in Hebrew. In English, however, it is the custom to refer to God as 'he', whether one is referring to God the Holy Trinity, or to God the Father, or to God the Son, or to God the Holy Spirit. This fits with the immense importance of the term 'Father', and with the maleness (according to His human nature) of Jesus, the Son of God. It is not meant to imply that God has a gender, nor that women are less in God's image than men are. I have chosen to refer to God as 'He', 'Him', etc., using a capital H. Besides being a traditional mark of reverence, this can serve to distance the pronouns used for God from the male overtones of the customary masculine pronouns.

Likewise, many languages have a word that means 'human being' and a different word that means 'male human being' (in Latin, *homo* as opposed to *vir*). In English, the word 'man' has in the past done duty for both meanings. Nowadays, this usage is liable to be misunderstood and can distract from the point being made; so I have avoided it where possible. I have retained the traditional usage in quotations, and have referred to Jesus as 'man'; but I have tried to find neutral terms in which to refer to human beings or to Christians in general. Where I have needed to use a single human being in some example, I have sometimes used a woman or girl, and sometimes a man or boy.

2 Baptism is the ritual washing by which people become Christians. In Augustine's time it was normally given only to adults, and to children who were in danger of death; but in earlier and later centuries it was regularly given to children.

3 Some of the Scriptures, or sacred writings, that make up the Bible, were written in Hebrew, and the rest in Greek influenced by Hebrewidiom. The Latin translations of these writings preserved that idiom, which seemed barbaric to those brought up on classical Latin literature.

4 Since two of the images used to express the Church's nature are 'Mother' and 'Bride of Christ', the Church can be referred to as 'she' and 'her'.

5 From the Roman Missal, ICEL translation.

6 My phrases 'at Christ's command' and 'from [her] beginning' do not imply that Jesus laid down precise, unalterable ritual rules for all the sacraments. In the case of some, practice has evolved considerably. The Church came to see that certain of the sacraments

were implicit in Jesus' words and deeds only after celebrating them for several centuries.

7 Some influential doctrinal statements have been put forward by local Councils, attended by bishops from one particular area. But an *Ecumenical Council*, in which the bishops represent the whole Church, and whose decrees the Pope confirms, has authority to declare what it is that the Church believes. The most recent Ecumenical Council was the Second Vatican Council, held 1962–65.

8 The greatest of St Thomas's many writings is the *Summa Theologiae* ('textbook of theology'). Its three parts tell how God makes and guides all things; how by the help of His grace we can journey towards Him; and how grace comes to us through Jesus and His sacraments. St Thomas asks one question after another, considering each time what objections there might be to his position. This reminds us of the limitations of our minds, which cannot focus on every detail and on the broad sweep of things all at the same time, and it encourages us to recognize truth wherever it may be found.

PART 1

---- ❧ ----

GOD OUR SOURCE AND
OUR GOAL

This part of the book sets out, first, the truth that
God is the Source of all that exists. Despite His
unimaginable greatness as the Creator, He has made us
in His own image, so that we can be truly fulfilled in
communion with Him. He has shown us something of
His life which He has called us to share, namely that
He is Father, Son and Spirit. The communion with
God we hope for is an entering into the relationships of
Father, Son and Spirit; its joy will overflow into our
risen bodies and into our communion with each other in
bliss.

CHAPTER 1

GOD THE CREATOR OF ALL THAT IS

CREATION

The existence of God the Creator can be known with certainty
through his works, by the light of human reason, even if this
knowledge is often obscured and disfigured by error . . . We
believe that God created the world according to his wisdom. It is
not the product of any necessity whatever, nor of blind fate or
chance. We believe that it proceeds from God's free will; he
wanted to make his creatures share in his being, wisdom and
goodness . . . God is infinitely greater than all his works . . . But
because he is the free and sovereign Creator, the first cause of all
that exists, God is present to his creatures' inmost being . . .
With creation God does not abandon his creatures to themselves. He not only gives them being and existence, but also, and
at every moment, upholds, and sustains them in being, enables
them to act and brings them to their final end . . .

(*Catechism of the Catholic Church*,
paragraphs 286, 295, 300, 301)

H UMAN beings are naturally inquisitive; we like to ask
questions about the world, and to try out various answers.
One reason modern science has developed is that lots of
questions have been asked and have been pursued so far that
important patterns have been discovered. Some people have
asked, and some still ask, very deep questions, of the kind that
scientific experiments cannot answer, but careful thought
might. Very roughly speaking, it is the job of *philosophers* to deal
with such questions.

Struck by the order and harmony of the world, which persist
despite the forces of destruction and chaos, the ancient Greek
philosopher Plato looked beyond this world for the source of its

recurring structures. His one-time disciple Aristotle looked to 'the Unmoved First Mover' for the continuing motion of things, which he did not think could be explained from within the world. Later Greek philosophers penetrated deeper, and, instead of asking about the order and movement of things in the world, they asked about their very *existence*. They were not content with the idea that stuff is already there for God to mould into patterns or to keep moving; they wanted to see God as the source of the *whole* of every thing – the matter in it, its structure, its movement, its goodness, its whole being. Every thing is complex in some way, and can fall apart. It moves, or changes in other ways. It is limited. And so, these philosophers said, every thing depends on some higher thing, to help it hold together, to help it develop; and the higher things are less limited. All things, no matter how great, depend on the highest of all, on God. God is not complex, and cannot fall apart, and so He does not need to be held together. God does not change or develop, but is already perfect; He is not limited. So God is not dependent on anything higher. He simply *is*; He exists in a higher way than all things, for all things receive their existence from God, but God does not need to receive His kind of existence from any other source.

This brief account does not do justice to the philosophers I have mentioned. But it illustrates how, by looking at the things around them, and noticing their limitations and dependencies, people who were not given the revelation contained in the Bible still achieved profound ideas about God. Nevertheless, it took many generations of great thinkers to arrive at these ideas; and other great thinkers have said that there is no God. Many great Christian, Jewish and Muslim thinkers have respected and used the ideas of the Greek philosophers, claiming that reason supports faith. But other thinkers – even great Christian ones – have doubted whether one can prove that God exists. Because the human mind is weak when faced with such deep questions, God has come to our help, and *revealed* Himself to us.[1] So, as the First Vatican Council, held in 1870, put it, because of 'this divine revelation, truths about God that are not of themselves beyond human reason can be known by everyone with ease, with firm certainty, and with no admixture of error' (*Dogmatic Constitution on the Catholic Faith*, 2).

You do not have to be a great thinker before you can say that the world is *created*, *made to be*, by God. You can read it in the Bible:

> Lift up your eyes on high and see: who created these? He who brings out their host by number, calling them all by name; by the greatness of His might, and because He is strong in power, not one is missing . . . The LORD is the everlasting God, *the Creator of the ends of the earth.*
>
> (Isaiah 40:26, 28)

The same sense of creatures pointing beyond themselves to the Creator is found in this passage from St Augustine:

> And what is this God? I asked the earth and it answered: 'I am not He'; and all the things that are in the earth made the same confession. I asked the sea and the deeps and the creeping things, and they answered: 'We are not your God; seek higher' . . . I asked the heavens, the sun, the moon, the stars, and they answered: 'Neither are we God whom you seek.' And I said to all the things that throng about the gateways of my flesh: 'You have told me of my God, that you are not He; so tell me something of Him.' And they cried out in a great voice; 'He made us.'[2]

As the Old Testament developed, God led the Jewish people to an ever deeper understanding of His greatness, and of how all that exists only exists because He makes it to. Independently of the Greek philosophers (and perhaps more sharply than they) the Jews knew how different God is from the complex, limited, changing things that depend on Him.

> To whom will you liken God? . . . For my thoughts are not your thoughts, neither are your ways my ways, says the LORD. For as the heavens are higher than the earth, so are my ways higher than your ways and my thoughts than your thoughts.
>
> (Isaiah 40:18, 55:8–9)

If the Bible emphasizes how God transcends the world, it also emphasizes His love and His care for it and for His people. The conviction that God has revealed Himself and His love to us makes us more ready to speak of God *choosing* to create the world, whereas the Greek philosophers tended to see it as coming from God in a less personal, almost automatic way. Some of them did seek some kind of mystical union with God;

we believe that God has 'drawn near' to us, making possible a union we could not achieve by merely human power.

St Thomas Aquinas brings out how every thing that exists depends on God the source of existence, every moment of its existence. In this way he holds together a profound sense of God's otherness, and a profound sense of God's love and closeness. For God is not dependent, and so He is radically different from creatures, which are dependent. God is not located within the world as we are, but He is present in everything as sustaining it by His will that it should exist. He loves it into existence – for when we love something or someone, we respond to the goodness that is there; but God's love for things and people *creates* the goodness that is in them, which is to say, it makes them to be, with all their strength and beauty.

For those who like to think in terms of diagrams, I offer the following analogy for the way in which the world depends on God. Two sets of diagrams are shown, of a kettle boiling on the gas (A), and of me choosing to eat some cake (B). Let them stand for all the things that happen in the world, those that happen because of physical laws, and those that happen by free choice. The question is, how should we fit God into the diagrams, how should we show God's relationship to the things and the events of this world?

An atheist would say that there is no need to put God into the diagrams. Let us simply show the gas heating the water, making it boil, and me deciding to eat the cake. Unless the notion of free choice is also to be rejected we can show that my choice is not forced by anything outside me. But God is not to be shown, for He has no part to play. This gives us the first diagram in each set.

By contrast, certain philosophers had so profound a sense of God's activity in the world that they thought He did everything in such a way that creatures did nothing. This view is represented by the second diagram, in which God boils the water and moves my limbs for me. St Thomas rejected that account, on the grounds that the world would be less good if its members had no role to play in what happens. It makes God too 'paternalistic'.

The third diagram shows a more refined sense of God's activity: God makes the gas to boil the water, and makes me choose to eat the cake. But there is still a sense in which He is

A

WRONG. The gas boils the water and God is not involved at all.

WRONG. God boils the water and the gas is not involved at all.

WRONG. God makes the gas act on the water as a puppeteer moves a puppet, and the gas does not exercise a power of its own.

RIGHT. As the paper supports the picture, so God makes the whole situation to exist: the gas, its power and its action on the water. God and the gas work at different levels, not in competition.

B

WRONG. I decide to eat the cake, and so I reach out for it with my hand; but God is not involved at all.

WRONG. God moves my hand to reach for the cake, and my will is not involved at all.

WRONG. God moves my will to a decision to eat (and so I reach out) as a puppeteer moves a puppet, and I do not exercise a power to choose cake, nor actualize a liking for cake.

RIGHT. As the paper supports the picture, so God makes the whole situation to exist: me, my power to decide, my liking for cake, my free decision, the consequent reaching out. God and I work at different levels, not compet-

like a puppeteer moving His creatures; they are not truly exercising their own powers. St Thomas insisted, however, that in His love and wisdom God gives His creatures what we might call 'structures' and 'strengths' so that they can truly act and express their natures in their activity.

God has been put into the second and third diagrams as if He were part of the world, so that when things happen He is exercising His influence alongside the influence of other causes, or even in competition with them. The correct way of drawing the diagrams is to do what the atheist wants to do, and keep God out of the diagrams! So in the fourth diagram we return to the way the diagrams were drawn first. But we note an important point, which had not struck us before. The diagrams are drawn on paper. Without the paper to support them, they could not be. The paper is not part of them, but it is essential to them. That is an analogy for the way it is with God. He is not part of the world, but He sustains it in being. He has been called our 'ground of being'. We are held in being, all that is is held in being by God, by His creative love.

So when the kettle boils, God is not at work alongside the gas. Rather, as the whole diagram of the gas boiling the water rests on the paper, so the gas, the water, the heating power of the gas and its action on the water are all made to be by God. Every thing that exists, with its structure, its strengths, its activities, depends totally on God. But because He gives being to the whole world, with all the causal relationships in it, He is not 'in competition with His creatures', like a parent reluctant to give a child some independence. Also, science has a valid role, namely to discover the natures of things, their structures, strengths, activities and relationships. All that it discovers is made to be by God.

The paper is quite different from the diagram it supports, and is present beneath every bit of the diagram. God is quite different from the world He creates, and is present in every bit of it, in every thing and every action that is at all real. Of course my analogy does not do justice to God's otherness. For example, the diagram should not be seen as suggesting that God is somehow the space within which things happen. To measure space or time, is to measure certain aspects of how things relate to each other. Space and time are made to be by God, in His action of making things to be.

If we can achieve a profound sense of God's otherness, our sense of wonder can be deepened when we consider those ways in which, after all, God *does* come to dwell in this world. I am not referring to miracles, but to what is greater – the life of Jesus Christ, the sacrament of Holy Communion, and God's presence in those who love Him. If we are to avoid naïve ways of thinking of God's presence, still more are we to avoid being blind to the mysterious closeness of the incomprehensible God.

Some thinkers have seen God as a 'watchmaker' who set up the universe with its laws at the beginning of time, then left it to run itself. As Stephen Hawking puts it:

> With the success of scientific theories in describing events, most people have come to believe that God allows the universe to evolve according to a set of laws and does not intervene in the universe to break these laws. However, the laws do not tell us what the universe should have looked like when it started – it would still be up to God to wind up the clockwork and choose how to start it off.[3]

But God's 'work' as Creator is much more than that: He is present to every thing *all the time, making it to be, sustaining it in existence*. He cannot leave the world to run itself – if He left it, it would cease to exist. So it would not be enough for God to 'intervene' in history just now and then – He is present all the time, creating and guiding the whole of history.

Hawking's theories suggest that it is not meaningful to speak of a 'first moment' when the universe sprang into being. Perhaps the laws that govern the development of the universe also determine its conditions at what we call the beginning of time. So God did not have to choose how to start the universe off. Still, a theory

> is just a set of rules and equations. What is it that breathes fire into the equations and makes a universe for them to describe? The usual approach of science of constructing a mathematical model cannot answer the questions of why there should be a universe for the model to describe.[4]

The answer to the questions is that *God* makes the universe that the equations describe.

I could enlarge my diagrams to show several events that happen in the course of time, or several things that are separated in space. But one piece of paper would support my representations of what is spread out in time and space. This may serve as an analogy for how the whole universe, throughout all its dimensions, depends on the transcendent God. In what may be envisaged as one creative act He makes it to be, spread out as it is through both space and time. In God himself there is neither space nor time; no change and development, but a life of unimaginable intensity and richness, which we can call God's *eternity*.

As the universe develops, and as our own lives unfold, some things are determined to happen by physical laws, some happen by chance, and some we freely choose. Not all that happens is determined by the laws of nature. The diagrams show water whose boiling was determined by the gas, and a choice to eat that was mine and not determined by anything outside me. But all that happens is made to be by God; it comes about as He wills. Therefore we can trust in His loving *providence*, His wise guidance of things. This does not mean we can ignore the physical laws that operate in this world, or sit back and do nothing. It is through the powers He has given things, and through our work, that God accomplishes much of what is to be accomplished. Now and then, a *miracle* occurs. This is not an intervention of a God who is normally absent – He is present all the time – but the absence of a cause within the world. A sudden healing without medical help, or the raising of a dead person, might speak to us of the power of God – but only because they are out of the ordinary. Our lives, our health, and medical skill, also speak to us of the power of God, but we so take them for granted that we forget to listen.

RECOGNIZING AND CHERISHING WHAT GOD HAS CREATED

Each of the various creatures, willed in its own being, reflects in its own way a ray of God's infinite wisdom and goodness. Man must therefore respect the particular goodness of every creature, to avoid any disordered use of things which would be in contempt of the Creator and would bring disastrous consequences for human beings and their environment . . . The existence of the spiritual, non-corporeal beings that sacred Scripture usually

calls 'angels' is a truth of faith . . . As purely *spiritual* creatures
angels have intelligence and will: they are personal and immortal
creatures, surpassing in perfection all visible creatures.

(*Catechism* 339, 328, 330)

The first chapter of the Bible presents the world as a home for
living things and especially for us. It was probably written
down while the Jews were in exile in Babylon, to help them
keep faith in their God, so different from the 'gods' of the
nations that seemed to be stronger. Those 'gods', often
associated with the heavenly bodies, needed and demanded the
service of human beings. But the true God has no need of
anything, and simply out of love provides generously for us who
need Him. He does ask His people to worship Him – but that is
because knowing and worshipping our Creator is good *for us*.

We know now how much more vast the universe is than the
first authors of Genesis supposed, its great extent through space
and time reflecting the immensity of God. Though good in
itself, it is also good as the home God has designed for us. We
can only survive because the conditions on this planet have been
right for the development of life, and those conditions depend
on the history of the whole universe being right. So while we
praise God for the wonders of His creation, we can also see in
them a sign of His care for us. We can enjoy the world, so long
as we do so in a reasonable way, not foolishly or greedily. Since
it is our home, we should cherish and respect it, which implies a
wise stewardship and places limits on how we may exploit the
world's resources. Because it is given to the human race for the
well-being of all, its resources should be shared out justly both
within and between nations. We may make use of other species
of living things, for our food and for other benefits, just as they
make use of each other; but that does not justify wasteful
farming methods or agricultural policies, and it is not right that
some should eat more richly than is healthy while others cannot
obtain a basic diet. Nor is cruelty justified, which demeans us.

The correct attitude to creation is expressed by *thanksgiving*.
It is an admirable custom to ask God's blessing on ourselves and
our food before eating, and to thank Him for it afterwards.
Christians have inherited this custom from the Jews, who pray,
for example:

Blessed art Thou, O Lord our God, Creator of the fruit of the
vine . . . Blessed art Thou, O Lord our God, who bringest forth
bread from the earth.

The night before He died, Jesus celebrated a solemn meal with
His closest followers, and gave thanks over bread and wine in
the traditional way, adding 'This is my Body . . . ' and 'This is
the cup of my blood . . . '. So He gave us our greatest act of
worship, the Holy 'Eucharist' (which means 'thanksgiving') or
Holy Communion. In the course of this service, the priest takes
bread and wine and gives thanks over them, repeating Jesus'
words. This shows us, among much else, the goodness of
creation. The bread and wine, which represent both natural
things and human life and work, are made use of by God so that
He can approach us with yet greater gifts. One prayer
sometimes used at the Eucharist runs:

> Father, all-powerful and ever-living God, we do well always and
> everywhere to give you thanks. All things are of your making, all
> times and seasons obey your laws, but you chose to create man in
> your own image, setting him over the whole world in all its
> wonder. You made man the steward of creation, to praise you
> day by day for the marvels of your wisdom and power, through
> Jesus Christ our Lord. We praise you, Lord, with all the angels,
> in their song of joy . . .

(Fifth Preface for Sundays *per annum*)[5]

This prayer ends with a mention of the *angels*. Although the
earlier references to 'angels' in the Bible are of an obscure
nature, it is clear that the authors of the New Testament
believed that God had made spiritual beings that do not live in
this material world, but can be sent to us with messages and
other help ('angel' means 'messenger'). They also believed that
some of these beings had rebelled against God and now seek to
harm us and spoil God's work. In the Church's prayers, the
worship we offer to God is seen as blending with that offered by
the faithful angels who enjoy God's company:

> As the unique Good and Fount of life you have made all things,
> so as to fill your creatures with blessings and to give many of
> them the joy of the vision of your light. And so innumerable
> hosts of angels stand before you, who serve you night and day
> and, as they gaze upon the glory of your face, glorify you

unceasingly. With them we too, and, through our voice, every
earthly creature, proclaim your name with rejoicing.

(Preface to Eucharistic Prayer IV)[6]

The Church believes that the rebellious angels, led by Satan
(also called 'the Devil'), exist; but we should not try to diagnose
their influence on events in an unhealthy, morbid way – rather,
we should trust in God's all-powerful and loving guidance of
our lives.

St Thomas Aquinas saw the angels as having a higher kind of
life than we do, because they possess very powerful faculties of
mind and will. They are able to know and to love in an
unimaginably intense way, not needing to gather sense data and
interpret it by a reasoning process as we do. Therefore they do
not need or possess bodies, and are not subject to the limitations
of life within time and space.

The existence of the angels brings home to us the creative
power of God, who has made more kinds of things than we can
fathom. It reminds us of our limitations, for not only can we not
understand the angels; we also have a much lower way of being
and of knowing than they do, and should recognize how much
we, by contrast, have in common with the rest of the animal
kingdom of which we are part. Our minds need to be nourished
with sense data; we can only develop our ideas with the help of
language and imagery. The existence of the angels also brings
home to us the generosity of God, since they were created so
that they might enjoy a share in God's life and happiness.

HUMAN NATURE

The human person . . . is a being at once corporeal and spiritual
. . . In Sacred Scripture the term 'soul' often refers to human *life*
or the entire human *person*. But 'soul' also refers to the
innermost aspect of man, that which is of greatest value in him
. . . 'soul' signifies the *spiritual principle* in man . . . The unity of
soul and body is so profound that one has to consider the soul to
be the 'form' of the body: i.e., it is because of its spiritual soul
that the body made of matter becomes a living, human body;
spirit and matter, in man, are not two natures united, but rather
their union forms a single nature. The Church teaches that every
spiritual soul is created immediately by God – it is not
'produced' by the parents – and also that it is immortal: it does

not perish when it separates from the body at death, and it will
be reunited with the body at the final Resurrection.

(Catechism 362–366)

Of all God's creatures, we are the most complex. We possess the
faculties of the other animals, and the faculties of the angels,
but in the unique combination that makes up human life. Many
different views have been held, and are held, about human
nature. Some are not compatible with the Christian faith; others
have been used by various Christian thinkers as they have
sought to set out their faith. However, if we can be as accurate
as possible in our understanding of ourselves, we will find it
easier to see the point both of Christian hope and of Christian
moral teaching.

For some thinkers, human beings, like other animals, are
nothing more than material bodies, and thought is nothing
more than chemical processes in the brain. For others, human
beings are made up of two very different kinds of things: a
material body behaving according to physical laws, and a
spiritual soul which is basically the same kind of thing as an
angel. Sometimes the body is seen as a kind of prison from
which the soul is meant to escape; some people believe in
reincarnation, supposing that the soul passes at death from one
body to another body, even one of a different species. All these
views are inadequate, some of them seriously misleading.

One problem with all these views is that they are too simple,
for they do not recognize the variety of things that exist. One
view recognizes only matter; the others recognize both matter
and spirit. If one only recognizes the existence of matter,
behaving according to physical laws, it becomes difficult to
account for the achievements of human culture, and even for
our ability to stand back from the 'here and now' and think in
general terms – an ability that even simple uses of human
language bear witness to. If one supposes that the human being
consists of two entities awkwardly held together, one fails to do
justice to the unity-in-diversity of our life and consciousness.

St Thomas Aquinas recognized not one, or two, but very
many kinds of being, ranging from inanimate objects to angels,
and each existing in its own way. He expressed both the unity of
the human being and our place in the scheme of things by
saying that the rational *soul* is the 'form' of the human body, an

expression sanctioned by the Council of Vienne (1311–12). We might understand the soul of a plant or animal as its 'form of life', which is expressed in its bodily structure, and lies behind the range of faculties it manifests. We may then contrast the human 'form of life', the human soul, with that of the higher animals. We have much in common with them, such as abilities to receive and organize sense data, and emotions; but we have extra faculties, called 'intellect' and 'will', by which, as we shall see, we transcend the limitations of the material. We express our possession of those faculties by calling our soul 'rational'; they form an organic whole with our other faculties.

My human body, then, is not an object that exists independently of my soul, and which my soul somehow dwells within and tries to control. The organic, living structure of my body is what my soul is responsible for; in St Thomas's technical sense of the word, the soul 'forms' the body. But it does not fully express itself in doing this, since it has those faculties that transcend the material. That is to say, not all my life is lived through bodily organs. Although I live one life, it is not an entirely bodily life. Therefore, unlike the life of plants and the other animals, it is not brought to an end by bodily death. Our souls, unlike those of other animals, survive, though they only retain the faculties of intellect and will.

Not just the way in which our life transcends the lives of other animals, but also the way in which it overlaps with theirs, can help us see that 'artificial intelligence' is a very limited model for human intelligence. A computer is a machine, made up of components each complete in itself, arranged in such a way that the user can run certain programmes on it. An animal is an organism, a single whole, whose organs can only be what they are as part of a living body. It does not need a user in order to have meaning and value; it has a certain spontaneity, a power of self-movement. If an animal brain and an animal body are a different kind of thing from computer circuits in their casing, how much more does human life surpass the workings of a computer.

In the light of this view of human nature, we can say that whenever a new human being is conceived, a special creative act of God is exercised. God is of course at work in all His creatures and on every occasion something new comes to be. But He is at work more powerfully when a human being comes into existence, since what is produced, being more than a bodily being, is more than a product of biological forces.

Likewise God communicates with us in ways that suit the nature He has given us: through the coming among us as man of God the Son; through the words and images of the Bible; and through the words, gestures and material elements of the sacraments. Our worship of God is expressed in word and music and gesture, and is offered in common as well as privately. Our obedience to God involves what we do with our bodies, and not just 'interior attitudes'; for we must respect and cherish our whole selves, and the whole selves of those around us.

Finally, since the human soul survives death with its faculties of intellect and will, it is possible for those who die as God's friends to know Him and rejoice in His love, while those who die as His enemies can torment themselves over losing Him. But the completion of God's work involves the resurrection of the body, so that His friends can enjoy eternal bliss as whole human beings, not disembodied souls. The mere survival of the soul after death is not a source of hope: left to itself, a disembodied soul would endure a truncated 'grey' existence. It is the promise of the vision of God, and of the resurrection, that gives us hope, and urges us to live in such a way as not to reject that promise.

MADE IN THE IMAGE OF GOD

> The human person participates in the light and power of the divine Spirit. By his reason, he is capable of understanding the order of things established by the Creator. By free will, he is capable of directing himself towards his true good. He finds his perfection 'in seeking and loving what is true and good'. By virtue of his soul and his spiritual powers of intellect and will, man is endowed with freedom, an 'outstanding manifestation of the divine image'.
>
> (*Catechism* 1704–1705)

The Bible (Genesis 1:26) represents God as deciding to make human beings 'in our image', and Christian thinkers have made much of this notion that we are in the image of God. Often it has been associated with our possession of intellect and will, which have been seen as a pale reflection of God's own power to know

and to love. That is, in His wisdom God has made a world of
beauty, an Artist or Architect expressing Himself in His work;
and He has given us power to investigate the structures of the
world and appreciate its beauty. In His love God has made good
things to exist, notably human beings, and He has given us the
ability to respond to the goodness around and within us.

> Man judges rightly that by his intellect he surpasses the material
> universe, for he shares in the light of the divine Mind.
>
> (Vatican II, *Pastoral Constitution on the
> Church in the Modern World*, 15)[7]

With our *intellect* we can stand back from our immediate
situation, our position in space and time, and acquire and use
abstract knowledge. A scientist may come to know the life-
pattern of newts by performing experiments in a particular
laboratory, on certain individual newts, during a particular
year. But her knowledge will leave behind those elements of
particularity – she may even forget what experiments she
performed – and her understanding of what a newt is, her
universal concept of 'newt', will apply equally well to newts in
her own country or abroad, to present-day newts or newts of the
past or future. In fact, much human thought, not just scientific
thought, employs universal concepts. It is expressed in *language*, in which sounds or shapes, grasped by the senses and the
imagination, convey meanings grasped by the intellect, and in
which ideas are organized and developed. Language is a social
reality, developed by and cementing society. Many of the
aspects of the complex whole that is human nature are
embodied in human language. With a few sounds I can discuss
tonight's supper, or the nature of light, or the majesty of God.
From my place on a small planet near the end of the twentieth
century, I can range in my mind's eye over whether I have
watered my plants recently, over the first few seconds of the
universe's expansion, and over the nature of distant quasars.

The intellect allows us to grasp truth, and there is no
automatic limit to the number of truths we can learn, or to how
general they can be. Therefore the intellect is open to God
Himself, *the* Truth, the source of all truth. Our delight in
learning is a kind of thirst for God, the Cause of all. So the

image of God which we are, can come to its fulfilment and
perfection in the knowledge of God.

It is characteristic of us human beings to have goals for which
we can plan, which we can pursue with a creativity not shared
by the other animals. They have drives, of varying complexity,
which we also have in the form of a more subtle emotional life;
but we can also think about what is good, what is fulfilling, we
can hold to an order of priorities based on reason, we can make
decisions in the light of principles and so stand back from the
here-and-now possibilities of pleasure and pain. That is to say,
we have a *will*. We can decide to give up some gratification for
the sake of future health or moral principle, although much of
what might be called our 'moral project' is concerned with the
education, not the suppression, of our emotions.

Because of this capacity to stand back from the here-and-now
in thinking and deciding, our behaviour is not fully determined
by our environment or our inheritance: we enjoy *freedom*. That
is, we are masters of ourselves, responsible for what we do. This
mastery is acquired as we grow up and may be limited by
psychological disturbance. But, those factors apart, I may
choose to reflect upon my situation and upon what goals I wish
to pursue within it. In the diagram on page 17, my choice to eat
was not determined by anything in the world – but it did
depend on God, for freedom is not independence of God, it is a
sharing in His own limitless freedom and creativity, and grows
as we become attuned to His guidance.

Just as our intellect's openness to truth means that we are
open to the knowledge of God, so our will's openness to the
good means that we are open to the enjoyment of God, the
unlimited Good. With His help we can make Him our priority,
love Him above all things, journey towards Him, and so come
to rest eternally in Him, fulfilled in the sharing of His own bliss.

Since we share the faculties possessed by the plants and the
other animals, but can also speak and sing, so giving expression
to knowledge and love, we are called to be 'spokesmen' for the
material creation. As the quotation on pages 22–3 put it, it is
through our voice that every earthly creature proclaims God's
name. In us the material creation can reach a new dignity, for
God wishes to dwell in us as our Friend, and to bring us, body
and soul, to share His glory.

HOW DO WE TALK ABOUT GOD?

Since our knowledge of God is limited, our language about him is equally so. We can name God only by taking creatures as our starting point, and in accordance with our limited human ways of knowing and thinking . . . we can name God by taking his creatures' perfections as our starting point, 'for from the greatness and beauty of created things comes a corresponding perception of their Creator'.

(Catechism 40–41)

As creatures of flesh and society, who learn from the world and from each other, we are told about God by the words, deeds and sufferings of Jesus Christ, which are brought home to us by the sacraments and by the poetry and imagery of the Scriptures. These enable us to speak to God and about Him, but we must listen to them with care, and bear in mind how limited is our language for talking about the Creator, who is unimaginably different from His creatures. Our concepts are limited realities in our minds, by which we grasp the limited realities around us. By no concept can we grasp the nature of God; He defeats our minds as the sun defeats our power of sight. We can cope with truths, but not with the Truth Himself, unless, as we shall see, He comes to our aid and lifts us up to a new and higher life with Him.

We can put this another way. Consider how many atoms there are in the universe. (There are about 70,000,000,000, 000,000,000,000,000 atoms in a pound of sugar; the sun weighs about 5,000,000,000,000,000,000,000,000,000,000,000 pounds; there are about 100,000,000,000 stars in our galaxy alone, many bigger than the sun . . . [8]) God knows the movements and rearrangements of each one of those atoms throughout the ten or twenty thousand million years of the universe's history, and their future movements. If you could imagine what kind of mind could hold that knowledge, you would have no better understanding of what God is than a child who imagines Him to be an old man with a beard! In fact you might have a worse understanding, for you might suppose that God is actually like that great mind you had imagined, whereas the child might happily accept that God is not really like the picture she has of Him. God is not like that great mind, because He does not just know things, He *makes them to be*. No created mind, however great, can make things *to be*.

In this life, then, we can readily say what God is not, we can with confidence say that He is not limited, not changeable, as creatures are. But God has said, through His Son and in Scripture, much that is positive about Himself and His ways. Necessarily, though, the Bible, and what we say to expound it, often make use of imagery. We read for example: 'The LORD is my rock and my fortress' (Psalm 18:2); 'The LORD is my shepherd' (Psalm 23:1); 'The LORD has bared His holy arm' (Isaiah 52:10); 'The LORD arose as though He had been asleep, like a strong man fighting-mad with wine' (Psalm 78:65 NJB); 'The LORD was sorry that He had made man on the earth, and it grieved Him to His heart' (Genesis 6:6). The very number of images employed by the Bible not only delights our feeling for poetry but also reminds us that we do not know God as He is, and so must use many complementary images. Likewise the 'earthiness' of much of the Bible's imagery also reminds us that it is no good trying to know what God is by conjuring up more 'noble' or 'spiritual' images.

We must not try to do without imagery, poetry, art and music when we speak to or about God. If the Bible, the word of God, can use imagery, so can preaching, and so can the most careful theology. All these are for human beings. But imagery can be taken too literally, and this can lead to difficulties in accepting the message it is designed to convey. We must provide complementary images that balance each other, and make the limitations of our images clear. We should also make careful use of more literal language to express certain truths about God and His ways. The Bible itself makes use of more literal language as well as of imagery. Such language need not be too dry or technical. But it still is limited in its own way.

If we forget that much of what is said about God is in the form of imagery that needs to be qualified, we can be misled. The last quotation in the previous paragraph but one spoke of God changing His mind about the creation of mankind, and if we are not careful we can suppose it is literally true that God changes, perhaps from love to anger when we offend Him, and from anger to love when we repent and He forgives. But in fact the 'wrath of God' is a metaphor, an important and useful image, that must not be taken too far. Unlike us, God cannot change, from love to anger and back, or in any other way. Our relationship with God can be broken off and then restored – but that is because *we* turn from *Him*, and must be brought back. When we turn away from God's love, we may see Him as angry: either because we are resentful towards Him; or because we have come to view His law as an unfair imposition; or because He is allowing us to suffer (perhaps just from interior turmoil because we are behaving foolishly in rebelling against God) in order to bring us to our senses. We can speak of God's anger, and fear it; but it is not a literal reality.

Some of what we say about God is not in the form of images. When I say 'The LORD is my rock', I can also say 'Of course, I was not talking literally: He is not really a huge piece of granite'. But when I say 'God is good', I cannot add 'Of course, I was not talking literally: God is not really good'. God literally is good, He literally is wise, and so on. But I do not know *what* God's goodness is; I am unable to fathom His wisdom. When I say 'God is good', I mean what I say – but I do not fully know what I mean! Even when we talk about creatures, we use the word 'good' flexibly. We speak of good dogs and good dinners – but good dinners do not run after sticks. Our word 'good' can be well used of God, for all goodness is a pale reflection of the unlimited goodness of God. So we can say, literally and truly, 'God is good'. But He is good in so much higher a way that we have no idea of what the goodness of God is. It would do us no good to imagine a bigger and better human being or angel. God is 'not on the same scale' at all.

When we speak of God's *love*, we are speaking literally. We cannot fathom the depth of God's love, or lay down laws for how it must operate. Jesus Himself does not make God comprehensible: He remains mysterious – but supremely worthy of our trust. So if we break off our relationship with God, we may speak of His anger; but we must also speak of, and hope in, His love. For this love continues towards us, changeless, even if we wander from God. Secure in the knowledge of God's love, we can hope and pray for forgiveness, for our relationship with God to be restored; and this is achieved by His love reaching in to draw us back to Him and make us His friends again. We have to use the language of human relationships if we are to speak of this, and so we speak of being forgiven. But in the case of human relationships, forgiveness may involve the offended person turning back in response to the repentance of the one who committed the offence. In the case of our relationship with God, when we have offended Him He turns us back to Himself, creating our repentance rather than responding to it, just as His love creates goodness, whereas ours responds to it. *He* puts aside *our* wrath. Therefore we do not need to wonder anxiously whether God has forgiven us: if we are concerned that our relationship with Him be mended, that is because His changeless love is already drawing us back; it is a sign that His forgiveness is working on us. Our turning away from evil back to God is the work of His love, in which we can trust securely.

An awareness of the vital role of imagery in the Bible should not lead us to suppose that the stories it contains are always symbolic stories with no basis in fact. Jesus did tell symbolic stories which we call 'parables'. Certain books of the Old Testament, such as Jonah and Tobit, may perhaps best be seen as lengthy parables. The Old Testament also records significant events, however, such as the liberation of God's people from Egypt. We should recognize a kernel of historical fact within its accounts, even though the events are presented in such a way as to show us their significance as God's saving acts, which could not be shown us by a bare description such as a non-believing onlooker might have given. The gospels record the most significant events of all time – the ministry, death and Resurrection of Jesus Christ. Small wonder if the gospel-writers should present these events in ways designed to show us their inner meaning. It would be a great wonder if the gospel-writers did not seek to be faithful to the historical realities of Jesus' life and death, and of the ways in which His Resurrection was revealed. For we are not saved by ideas couched in the form of symbolic stories, but by certain events. The gospel-writers knew that if Jesus did not die and rise again, the Christian faith was groundless. In bringing out the inner meaning of the saving events, the gospels show us the meanings that God, the guide of all events, has placed within those events. Human beings need story and imagery, powerful ideas to sustain our lives and our projects. But we live our lives in time, we are concerned to establish facts. In His wisdom God has given us the most powerful image of His love, to sustain us with hope in His promise. And He gave it to us at a particular time, in events not merely factual but stark: in the birth of His Son in poverty, and the death of His Son on a cross. We make the story of the historical Jesus our own story by an action deeply symbolic and very simple, by taking bread and wine and giving thanks as He did one night 2,000 years ago.

NOTES

1 We shall see that the chief reason why God had to reveal things to us is that there are important truths human reason cannot arrive at by itself.
2 *Confessions* X, vi, translated by F.J. Sheed (Sheed and Ward, 1945).
3 Stephen Hawking, *A Brief History of Time* (Bantam Press, 1988), p. 140.
4 Ibid., p. 174.
5 From the Roman Missal, ICEL translation. The phrase *per annum* ('through the year') refers to the weeks that fall outside the main seasons of the Church's year; they are sometimes called 'weeks in ordinary time'.
6 From the Roman Missal. I have used my own, more wooden, translation, not the official one.
7 *The Documents of Vatican II*, translation edited by Walter M. Abbott (Geoffrey Chapman, 1967).
8 I use these figures to create a general impression, aware that sugar contains carbon and oxygen, which have heavier atoms than the hydrogen and helium of the sun, and that atoms are composed of smaller particles, found separately in the sun.

CHAPTER 2

GOD THE HOLY TRINITY

THE ONE GOD IS FATHER, SON AND HOLY SPIRIT

Christians are baptized in the *name* of the Father and of the Son
and of the Holy Spirit: not in their *names*, for there is only one
God, the almighty Father, his only Son and the Holy Spirit: the
Most Holy Trinity. The mystery of the Most Holy Trinity is the
central mystery of Christian faith and life. It is the mystery of
God in himself. It is therefore the source of all the other
mysteries of faith, the light that enlightens them . . . [God's]
inmost Being as Holy Trinity is a mystery that is inaccessible to
reason alone or even to Israel's faith before the Incarnation of
God's Son and the sending of the Holy Spirit.

(Catechism 233–234, 237)

ONE of the Biblical texts most cherished by the Jews is
Deuteronomy 6:4 – 'Hear, O Israel: The Lord our God,
the Lord is one.' Muslims have a similar conviction of the unity
of God. The Christian faith, too, is a faith in the one only God,
the Creator of all that is. This faith can be supported by reason
since, as we have seen, philosophical arguments can be put
forward for the existence of the God on whom the universe
depends for its being.

In the Creeds, the summaries of our faith, Christians
proclaim that we believe in the Father almighty, in Jesus Christ,
His only Son, and in the Holy Spirit. Each of the Three we
acknowledge to be God. This part of the Christian faith does not
rest on any philosophical arguments, it rests on our conviction
that God has shown us this truth. We believe, then, in God who
is *Father, Son and Holy Spirit*, in God who is the *Holy Trinity*,
the Three who are One. This belief is absolutely central.
Besides determining the structure of the creeds, it pervades the

34

Christian life. We become Christians when we are baptized 'in the name of the Father, and of the Son, and of the Holy Spirit'. Many forms of public and private prayer begin 'in the name of the Father, and of the Son, and of the Holy Spirit'. When we sing the Psalms in the form of worship called 'the Divine Office', we end each one: 'Glory be to the Father, and to the Son and to the Holy Spirit'. In such ways, we show that the lives we offer to God in our worship are dedicated to the God who is Father, Son and Holy Spirit.

Cardinal Newman began one of his hymns: 'Firmly I believe, and truly, God is three and God is one'. The Christian claim that the Father is God, the Son is God, and the Spirit is God, can sound shocking to Jews and Muslims. Surely this claim is in flat contradiction to the truth that God is one? Surely it is nonsense for Christians to say that they have as uncompromising a belief in the unity of God as Jews and Muslims do? It is not nonsense; the truth that the Three are One goes beyond, but not against, reason.

The doctrine of the Holy Trinity is a mystery, a truth we may explore but not exhaust, like the ocean that yields up new treasures in unexpected depths. We must not dismiss it as some strange arithmetic according to which three into one will go; the Holy Trinity is not a puzzle to be solved, but a life to be lived. This truth about God has been shown us in the central events of history, in the coming among us of the Son and the coming of the Spirit into the hearts of His disciples. The Spirit who came to the infant Church 2,000 years ago still comes to give life to Jesus' followers, and the life He gives is a sharing in the relationship of love between the Son, Jesus, and the Father. The destiny towards which the Spirit leads us is a yet deeper and more glorious sharing in that relationship of love and joy.

The ways in which we express our faith in the Holy Trinity were hammered out in the course of centuries of thought and controversy. A look at this development will help show what the doctrine of the Trinity is. It is important to have some sense of the Trinitarian life of God before we go on to discuss the person and work of Jesus, and the Christian life, so that we may see more clearly who Jesus is, and how the Christian life is nothing less than a sharing in the life of the Holy Trinity.

When we consider the very being of God, His nature, we have to say that God is one. There is but one divine being, one divine life, one divine power. The mind of God is one; the will of God by which the world is loved into being is one. And all these are one with each other. We have different names for them, because in us there are different faculties for knowing, for loving and for acting on the world around us. But there is no such complexity in God, there is perfect singleness – not in the way in which a single-celled animal is less than a complex animal, but in the way the intense richness of God's life must far exceed our 'spread out' kind of life.

When we change our point of view and consider the *relationships* in God, then we have to speak of the Father, the Son and the Spirit. We would not know that there are relationships in God, if God had not shown them to us. But the coming of the Son into the world shows us that in the life of God He comes from the Father. The love and obedience with which Jesus fulfilled the mission given Him by the Father show us the relationship of love between Them in the inner life of God. The coming of the Holy Spirit into the world, sent by the Father and the Son, shows us that in the inner life of God, His eternal changeless life, the Holy Spirit comes from the Father and the Son.

It was in the fourth century that great theologians developed the concept of relationships between Father, Son and Spirit as a way of exploring the Church's faith in the Holy Trinity. Before then, various attempts had been made to set out this faith, but not all were successful. For example, the Sabellians denied that there was any distinction between Father, Son and Spirit in the inner life of God; those three names express three roles, three ways by which God relates to us. We call Him Father when we think of His work of creation, we call Him Son when we think of His becoming our Brother, we call Him Spirit when we think of His dwelling in our hearts. This idea was rejected by the Church, because it does not do justice to the relationships shown us in the gospels, in which the Son prays to the Father, and promises that He and His Father will send another Friend, the Holy Spirit, to be with us.

Other theologians made use of the ideas of the philosophers we call the 'middle-' and the 'neo-Platonists'. These saw the complex world coming forth from the One (their term for God) through one or more intermediate beings. Some Christian thinkers saw the Son of God, and the Holy Spirit, as such beings who came forth from God the Father as the first stage of the unfolding of creation from God. This emphasized too much the distinction between Father, Son and Holy Spirit, and involved the risk of seeing the Son and Spirit as not fully divine. In the case of some theologians these faults were balanced by a concern to show the unity of will between Father, Son and Spirit, and by other images. In the case of Arius, however, early in the fourth century, this model lay behind a denial of the divinity of the Son. Arius saw the Son as coming from the Father as His first and greatest creature, and the rest of creation as coming from the Father through the Son. The Father alone is God, the Son is a kind of great angel.

The First Ecumenical Council, the first great Council of Bishops with the authority to define the Church's doctrine, met at Nicaea in what is now Turkey in AD 325. In order to repudiate the ideas of Arius, the council declared that the Son is *homoousios*, of one being, with the Father. St Athanasius, Bishop of Alexandria, was the greatest defender of the Council's teaching in the decades of controversy that followed. He made it clear that the coming of the Son and the coming of the Spirit from the Father are something quite other than the coming of creation from God. The Son is *begotten, not made*. If God had not created a world at all, God would still be Father, Son and Spirit. The Three are distinct because of Their roles in relation to each other, independently of Their roles towards us. Speaking of the relationship between the Father and the Son (since the debate did not at first widen to cover the status of the Holy Spirit), St Athanasius says:

> They are two in that the Father is Father and not also Son; the Son is Son and not also Father; but the nature is one . . . and all that is the Father's is the Son's . . . For even if the Son is distinct from the Father, as His offspring, still as God He is identical with Him; He and the Father are one by specific and proper nature, and by the identity of the one godhead.[1]

It almost goes without saying that when the Church Fathers spoke of God the Father begetting His Son, they did not have the pagan myths in mind. In those myths, the gods had offspring more or less as human beings do, and sometimes a god would visit a mortal woman and beget a son. The coming of the

Son from the Father in the timelessness of God is incomprehensible and non-physical, even though human parenthood is a pale image of it. Jesus is truly the Son of God, not because He was divinely conceived of the Virgin, but because He is the eternal Son who took on the human way of being when He was conceived of her.

Three saints, Basil the Great, Gregory Nazianzen and Gregory of Nyssa, continued the defence of the full godhead of the Holy Spirit. They expressed the unity of Father, Son and Spirit as one God by pointing to the way in which the Three work together with one divine power and action. The same saints claimed that the Son and the Spirit can be truly divine even though They are truly distinct from the Father, by exploring Their relationships with the Father. The Father is from no other; the Son is from the Father as His Son; the Spirit is from the Father in a different way. An analogy used by Gregory Nazianzen is the biblical story of God forming Eve from one of Adam's ribs. Adam, Eve and Seth (their third son) are all human, but Seth is from Adam as a son, and Eve is from him in a different way. Father, Son and Spirit are divine, even though Son and Spirit are from the Father. Gregory of Nyssa points out that if you ask a gardener whether a certain tree was cultivated or grew wild, you are not asking what kind of tree it is. If we ask whether the Son is from the Father or exists of Himself, we are not asking whether or not He is divine. In nature, the Three are equal and one; in terms of origin, one is from another. Lest such images should lead us to overemphasize the distinctions between the divine Three, Gregory Nazianzen points out that with Them, 'there is no separation in time, or in will, or in power. These factors make us men a plurality, each individual at odds with himself and with others' [Oration 42, 15].[2]

A version of Gregory Nazianzen's analogy (Adam, Eve and Seth) is found helpful by some people today, who point out that a close-knit family of father, mother and child can work 'as a single unit'. By itself this analogy suggests too great a distinction between the divine Persons, so it needs to be balanced by other analogies. For example, a girl might say that her mother is also her teacher and her best friend; the one woman fulfils three roles towards the girl, and within the woman herself these three roles enrich each other. In God the three 'roles' exist in relationship to each other with vastly greater solidity, and would do so even if there were no creatures They might relate to.

By speaking of the *coming* of the Son and the Spirit from the Father, the great teachers of the fourth century did not at all mean that first the Father was alone, then He begot the Son, and then the Holy Spirit came from Him. That idea was Arius's, and was firmly rejected. We cannot easily do without language that seems to imply before-and-after in God, just as in human experience a father is older than his son. But we can recognize which aspects of our images and ideas must be left behind when we point them towards God.

St Augustine wrote about the Holy Trinity in the late fourth and early fifth centuries. He analysed the notion of 'relationship' so as to show that the presence of relationships within God does not at all compromise the singleness of God. He explored various images of the Trinity found in human nature, and in particular suggested that the human mind contains three faculties, memory, intellect and will – we might see those as the mind's powers to contain things, to understand things, and to love things. This image of God is to be brought to perfection in communion with God, in the state we call heaven. There the mind is to be filled with God, to know Him and to love Him perfectly, so that the three faculties will be equal in their attachment to God and distinct in their functioning, rather as Father, Son and Spirit are equal as God but distinct in Their relationships.

One of St Augustine's contributions was to tie the doctrine that God in Himself is the Trinity more closely to the events in which we are shown this truth about God. He had in mind such events as the Baptism of Jesus, when the Spirit was seen in the form of a dove and the Father's voice was heard declaring Jesus to be His beloved Son. We can only learn about the Trinity by working back from the events that reveal the Trinity. Therefore when Jesus appeared to His disciples on the evening after He rose from the dead, breathed on them, and said, 'Receive the Holy Spirit', this showed that, in the life of God Himself, the Spirit comes from the Son as well as from the Father. Basil and the two Gregorys had not been able to show how the Spirit and the Son are distinct from each other, when it is a relationship of one-from-another that tells the Son and the Father apart, and the Spirit also has a relationship of one-from-another with the Father. Augustine suggested that the Spirit has a relationship of one-from-another with the Son as well as the Father; He is from both. The Bible shows us this relationship not so much by a form of words as by recording a gesture of Jesus.

Augustine sees the very coming of Jesus among us, and the coming of the Spirit into the Church at her birth, as tied up with the coming of the Son from the Father and the coming of the Spirit from the Father and Son, in the eternal life of the Trinity. Because the Son is from the Father, we can say that the Son is *sent* by the Father to become man, and that as a man He has a mission from the Father. When the Son took on a human way of being, without losing His divine way of being, and dwelt among us as Jesus of Nazareth, this was a kind of projection into the world of the Son's coming from the Father. When, after His death and Resurrection, and in company with the Father, Jesus sent the Spirit upon his followers, this was a kind of extension into the world of the Spirit's coming from the Father and the Son within the changeless divine life. So, while we do not want to say that the coming of the Son and the Spirit from the Father is the first stage of the work of creation – rather, God is in Himself the Holy Trinity – we do want to say that the work of salvation is a kind of out-pouring of the Holy Trinity, designed to draw us into sharing the life and love of the divine Three.

The saints of the fourth century were concerned to teach accurately the truths God had been kind enough to reveal about Himself, the same truths earlier Fathers had been ministers of. They were also determined to make clear the grounds on which our Christian hope is based. The New Testament promises us a share in the nature of God. In a sense, the work of the Son and of the Spirit is to make us divine. If They possess the divine nature by right, They have power to give us a share in it. If They are not truly divine, Athanasius suggested, They do not have authority to bestow a share in so great a gift.

Basil and the two Gregorys used the Greek words *ousia* and *hypostasis* to help us speak about the Holy Trinity. With regard to *ousia*, God is perfectly one; with regard to *hypostasis*, He is Three. *Ousia* can be translated as 'nature', and *hypostasis* as 'individual being', but the fact that both can be translated as 'substance' or as 'being' reminds us of the mysteriousness of the Trinity. The use of these technical terms does not explain the Trinity. Writing in Latin, Augustine followed the custom of speaking of the one *essentia* (nature) of God, and the three *personae* (persons). He stated explicitly how inadequate our language is. This should be borne in mind when we hear of 'the three Persons in the one God'. To call Father, Son and Spirit 'the three divine Persons' does not at all imply that They are three larger versions of human persons. Each of us has his or her own mind; we often perform tasks separately from each other. But in God there is one divine mind, one divine power, one divine being, possessed fully by the Father, and by the Son, and by the Holy Spirit, not somehow parcelled out among Them.

On the other hand, it is in the development of our relationships with others that we come to discover ourselves as individual persons, and in community with others that we achieve much of our fulfilment. So the word 'person', applied to God, can remind us that the Three who are God are told apart by their relationships, and that the divine happiness consists in the communion of Father, Son and Spirit, abiding in each other and rejoicing in each other. We can then see the Trinity as shedding light on the community of the Church, on marriage and on all human communities. God is communion in love without rivalry, and while the unity of Father, Son and Spirit is greater than we can conceive, Their personal characteristics are more richly different than we can imagine. We who are less than God in our unity and in our diversity, reflect Him when different gifts and personalities contribute to a community in which they are cherished, or man and woman come together for their mutual and fruitful enhancement.

The names 'Father', 'Son' and 'Spirit' are not meant to be taken too simplistically, as if two were male people and one a kind of force. We shall see the value of the title 'Word' for the Son – it can help us avoid picturing the coming of the Son from the Father in too crude a way. But the titles 'Father' and 'Son' express the devotion with which the Son made man did the work His Father asked of Him, spoke on His Father's behalf, and showed us His Father's love. We can express our Christian dignity by saying we are given a share in Jesus' sonship, we are called to become the Father's children in and through His Son.

The sense of impetus the word 'spirit' can evoke points to the vigour with which God reaches into the hearts of His friends and helps them on their way to Him.

Before we go on to examine how the Scriptures show us the Holy Trinity, and to look more closely at the way in which the human mind is in the image of the Trinity, it may be helpful to see how a great poet tried to express the Trinity. In his *Divine Comedy* Dante describes an imaginary journey through Hell, Purgatory and Heaven. At the end of his journey he gazes on God, and

> Within Its depthless clarity of substance
> I saw the Great Light shine into three circles
> in three clear colours bound in one same space;
>
> the first seemed to reflect the next like rainbow
> on rainbow, and the third was like a flame
> equally breathed forth by the other two.[3]

He symbolizes the Trinity by the three circles that cover the same area, since the divine Persons each possess the same nature; and by picturing light flowing from one circle to another, and from those two to the third, he puts forward an analogy for how the full divine being is given by the Father to the Son and by the Father and the Son to the Holy Spirit. The flow of the divine being is also represented in the famous icon painted by Rublev, reproduced on the cover of this book. In Genesis 18, Abraham is visited by three men, whom he entertains, but their visit turns out to be a visit by the (one) Lord. With hindsight, Christians came to see this as a hint of the Trinity, and, especially among Eastern Christians, artists have represented the Trinity by three angels entertained by Abraham. Rublev depicted the scene with great serenity. The three angels can be assigned to the three divine Persons in different (not incompatible) ways. The inclination of the heads of two of the angels can suggest the flow of the divine being from the Father, its source, through the Son, to the Holy Spirit. On the table at which the angels are seated is (as often in such icons) a cup, to show that we are called to share in the divine being, to enter into communion with the Blessed Trinity, and that the great help to doing this is the Holy Eucharist.

JESUS IS THE SON AND WORD OF THE FATHER

We believe and confess that Jesus of Nazareth . . . is the eternal
Son of God made man. He 'came from God' [John 13:3] . . . For
'the Word became flesh and dwelt among us . . . ' [John 1:14]
. . . Jesus performed acts, such as pardoning sins, that mani-
fested him to be the Saviour God himself . . . The New
Testament uses [the] full sense of the title 'Lord' both for the
Father, and – what is new – for Jesus, who is thereby recognized
as God himself. Christ, the Son of God made man, is the
Father's one perfect and unsurpassable Word. In him he has
said everything.

(*Catechism* 423, 594, 446, 65)

When the Fathers of the Church taught that in God's eternity
the Son is from the Father, and is equal to Him in godhead,
power and majesty, they were seeking to preserve intact what is
taught us in the Bible. Did they succeed? The Church hails
Jesus Christ as 'true God and true man', for the Son came
among us as man without ceasing to reign as God with the
Father. Where did she get her faith from? For the Bible only
calls Jesus 'God' a few times. In John 1:1 and 20:28 we read 'In
the beginning was the Word, and the Word was with God, and
the Word was God . . . Thomas answered Him, "My Lord and
my God!"'. Hebrews 1:8 quotes Psalm 45:6 – 'Of the Son He
says "Thy throne, O God, is for ever and ever"'. There are four
other passages where Jesus may be called 'God' but the correct
translation of the Greek is disputed. Jesus is not reported to
have said 'I am God'. Have we enough evidence for so central a
doctrine?

Note, first, that we should not be surprised to find that Jesus
is rarely called 'God' in the New Testament. For in the pagan
world of that time there were stories of many 'gods', some of
whom made visits to earth in various forms. It would not have
helped people brought up on such myths understand who Jesus
is if they had thought He was being presented as a god of that
kind. And before the Christian message was spoken to pagans,
it was spoken to Jews. Calling Jesus 'God' might have reminded
them of those pagan stories, or of the divine pretensions of
pagan rulers. Or, some commentators on the New Testament
suggest, it would have been too harsh an affront to their faith in

the unity of the true God. The statement 'Jesus is God' would not have been particularly helpful in the first century.

Second, we must realize that, under God's guidance, the Church could have reached correct conclusions about who Jesus is even if His own words, and the writings of His first followers, did not make any clear claims about His godhead.

Third, however, if we read the New Testament carefully, we do find the claim made that Jesus is divine. This can be more clearly seen if we are aware of the ways in which some Old Testament themes and first-century Jewish concepts are employed in the New Testament. The claim is implicit in the behaviour reported of Jesus, and in some of the reflection on Him that the New Testament contains. To my mind it was also made verbally by Jesus, by means of expressions whose implications were not always so obvious as to affront His hearers straight away, but were clear enough to provoke faith or enmity. In John's Gospel (10:33) we hear Jesus accused of 'blasphemy; because you, being a man, make yourself God'. Many commentators would see such a passage as deriving from reflection by the gospel-writer on Jesus' identity and persecution. But given, for example, that Mark's Gospel says Jesus was condemned for blasphemy (14:64), it seems to me likely that controversy over Jesus' claims did contribute to His being persecuted.

In Mark 2:1–12, Jesus forgives a man's sins, and some of the onlookers accuse Him of blasphemously claiming an authority that belongs to God. In the course of the 'Sermon on the Mount' (Matthew 5 – 7), He says, six times, 'You have heard that it was said . . . but *I* say to you . . . '. In this and similar ways Jesus claims authority with regard to the Law God had given. He 'steps into the space reserved for God'.

In Mark 4:41, Jesus is seen to have power to command the elements. In 6:45–51, He walks on the water, and Mark tells us 'He meant to *pass by* them', using language reminiscent of God's self-manifestation to Moses in Exodus 34:6. The miracles of Jesus in which, with His own word of command, He heals those subject to debilitating illnesses and even raises the dead, reveal a supernatural power.

God was held to have revealed His Name YHWH[4] to Moses (Exodus 3:14–15 and 6:3). By Jesus' time this name was only pronounced in the course of the Temple service. Otherwise it was replaced either by 'The Name' or by *Adonai* ('my Lord'). In the Greek translation of the Old Testament it was rendered by *Kyrios* ('Lord'). In the gospels, Jesus is addressed as *Kyrios*, and quite often this title should be translated as 'Sir'. Sometimes in the New Testament it is a much more honorific title, as when Stephen prays 'Lord Jesus, receive my spirit' (Acts 7:59). In passages such as 1 Corinthians 12:3 – 'Jesus is Lord!' – it is probable that Jesus is being given the title that belongs to God.

At the beginning of St John's Gospel we read of the Word who was with God, who is God, and through whom all things were made. Then: 'The Word became flesh and dwelt among us.' This title of Jesus, 'the Word', has been very important for Christian theologians. Because of the role the term *Logos* ('Word') played in Greek philosophy, some early theologians thought of the Son, the Word, as coming from the Father as the first stage of the unfolding of creation from its source. We saw how that notion was effectively abandoned; but the title 'Word' has inspired other ways of envisaging the coming of the Son from the Father. However, the first verses of John's Gospel rely on the Old Testament, Jewish use of 'Word', not on Greek philosophy.

At the beginning of the Old Testament, God is depicted speaking His creative commands. God said 'Let there be light' – and there was light. Psalm 33:6 reads 'By the word of the Lord the heavens were made'. Recounting the miracles by which God set His people free from Egypt, Wisdom 18:15–16 says 'Thy all-powerful Word leaped from heaven'. In Isaiah 55:10–11, God says 'As the rain and the snow come down from heaven, and return not thither but water the earth, making it bring forth and sprout . . . so shall my word be that goes forth from my mouth; it shall not return to me empty, but it shall accomplish that which I purpose . . . '. In these texts, it is not implied that there is some great creature called 'the Word', which carries out missions on behalf of God. Rather, a literary device is being used to safeguard God's transcendence. It is God Himself who is at work in creation, in the liberation of His people, and in the guidance of world events. But none of these exhausts the full riches of God's power. By speaking of the activity of God's *Word*, the Old Testament creates a sense of God's hiddenness: His works do not fully reveal His majesty. So when the Old Testament speaks of 'the Word of the Lord' it is speaking of

God Himself, performing deeds which express His purpose yet
leave His greatness unfathomed.

When Jesus is called 'the Word' in John's Gospel, this amounts
to a claim that Jesus is God, come among us to express – and to
accomplish – the divine purpose, but in such a way that the
blinding fullness of God's majesty is not shown to us unveiled.
In the human life and ministry of Jesus, God is with us; but (as
the Church was to say later) His manhood is less than His
godhead.

While the Old Testament does not imply that the Word is a
creature separate from God, St John's Gospel introduces a new
dimension: the Word is from the Father as His Son. The
relationship between the Word and the Father was not revealed
in Old Testament times; but, under God's guidance, the
authors of the Old Testament put forward certain ideas that
could be used in New Testament times to express who Jesus is.
These ideas had to be 'stretched' in order to capture something
of what was newly revealed about God. Later, creative thinkers
like St Athanasius were to stretch ideas drawn from other
backgrounds in order to preach the same truth about Jesus, God
from God and God who came to be with us.

We could reinforce what has been said about the implications
of calling Jesus 'the Word', by looking at other terms used in the
Old Testament and in first-century Jewish thought to express
the presence and activity of the incomprehensible God. For
example, Jesus is also presented in the New Testament as the
Wisdom, Name and *Shekhina* ('dwelling') of God.

On several occasions we read of Jesus saying '*I am*' with
solemnity. For example:

> You will die in your sins unless you believe that *I am He*.
> When you have lifted up the Son of Man, then you will know
> that *I am He*.
> Before Abraham was, *I am*.
> Jesus said to them, '*I am He*' . . . they drew back and fell to the
> ground.
>
> (John 8:24, 8:28, 8:58, 18:5–6, italics added)

The Greek for 'I am' or 'I am he' is *egō eimi*, which can also
mean 'It's me'. Maybe in the last of the above quotations the
phrase has this ordinary meaning. At least in the others, we are
meant by the gospel-writer to recall God's self-manifestation to

Moses in Exodus 3:14, which in its Greek version uses the phrase *egō eimi*. It is often supposed by modern scholars that the author of John's Gospel employed this device as a way of expressing Jesus' divinity, and that Jesus did not speak in this way. However, we find the same phrase in St Mark's Gospel:

> He spoke to them and said, 'Take heart, *it is I*'.
> Again the High Priest asked Him, 'Are you the Christ, the Son of the Blessed?' And Jesus said '*I am* . . . ' And the High Priest . . . said, 'Why do we still need witnesses? You have heard his blasphemy.'
> (Mark 6:50, 14:61–64, italics added)

Maybe we do have, after all, a record of Jesus' own way of speaking, a way which contained a veiled claim to divinity. Of course, He would not have been speaking in Greek. The Aramaic equivalent would have been *ana hu* (literally 'I he'). This would have been reminiscent not so much of Exodus 3:14 as of the several occasions in Isaiah where God is represented as saying (in Hebrew) *ani hu*. John 8:28, quoted above, echoes Isaiah 43:10: ' . . . that you may . . . understand that I AM HE.' In Jewish thought this expression *ani hu* was connected with the divine name revealed to Moses.

Whether or not Jesus actually said 'I am He', He certainly did address God as *Abba*, 'Father', with a unique sense of intimacy and dependence, and spoke of Himself as 'the Son', with a unique sense of sharing His Father's authority and life-giving work. In the Old Testament, the term 'son of God' is used for angels, for the king, for the whole of God's people, and for the righteous man. If it were the only title used of, or claimed by, Jesus, it might only imply dignity, authority and closeness to God. But it was understood by Jesus' enemies as well as by his friends to mean more than that:

> . . . the Jews [i.e., Judean authorities[5]] sought all the more to kill Him, because He . . . called God His Father, making Himself equal with God. Jesus said to them, 'Truly, truly, I say to you, the Son can do nothing of His own accord, but only what He sees the Father doing; for whatever He does, that the Son does likewise. For the Father loves the Son, and shows Him all that He Himself is doing . . . For as the Father raises the dead and gives them life, so also the Son gives life to whom He will . . . that all may honour the Son even as they honour the Father.

He who does not honour the Son does not honour the Father
who sent him.'

(John 5:18–23)

This title, 'Son', is one of great richness. Besides its warmth,
and the way it expresses the relationship between God the
Father and the divine Word, into which we are to be drawn, it
also holds together the godhead and the humanity of Jesus
Christ, true God and true man. For we can say that in the
Blessed Trinity the Word comes from the Father as His Son,
because He is from the Father and like the Father, and
in human relationships a son is from and like his father. But
we can also say that when the Word became flesh and dwelt
among us He lived out in a human way what it is to be Son of
God. In Jesus' ministry we see a translation into human form
of His eternal, divine sonship. In His human mind and heart
there are a knowledge, love, dependence and obedience towards
His Father, which enflesh that relationship in which the Son
receives the divine being from the Father and is perfectly one
with the Father. The fulfilment of the mission the Father gave
Jesus is the earthly expression of His coming from the Father
within the life of the Trinity. That coming was 'projected' into
the world of time when the Father sent the Son among us.

In Western Christian art the Holy Trinity is rarely represented by the three angels whom Abraham entertained. Often,
as in the picture reproduced on the front cover of this book, the
Father is shown as 'the Ancient of Days' of Daniel 7:9, and the
Son is shown, crucified, held in His Father's arms.[6] This is not
to imply that it is in His godhead that the Son died. It does
imply that the best picture we have of the sonship of the divine
Word is His death as man on the cross. When St John tells us
that 'the Word became flesh', he adds 'we have beheld His
glory, glory as of the only Son from the Father'. It becomes
clear that *the* hour of Jesus' glory is when He is lifted up on the
cross. That is when He is most clearly seen as the Son who does
His Father's work, who is obedient to His Father's will, who
reflects His Father's kindness, who reveals His Father's love. If
we are to be the Father's children, we must share the self-giving
love Jesus showed in His death on the cross. Then we can hope
to abide with Him in 'the bosom of the Father'.

Prompted by the title, 'Word', for the Son, St Augustine

suggested that the workings of the human mind might provide a helpful image for the coming of the Son from the Father. A thought can arise in the depths of my mind, which I then try to find words for, and eventually express in speech. The Son comes from the Father in the depths of God's eternity, and is sent to take flesh in time as the Father's speech to us.

> Whoever can understand [what] a word [is], not just before its sound is made, but even before the process of thought has unfolded the imagination of its sound . . . can already see in this mirror . . . some likeness of that Word of which it is said: In the beginning was the Word, and the Word was with God, and the Word was God.
>
> (*De Trinitate* XV, 10, 19; author's translation)

While Augustine saw our faculties of memory, intellect and will as reflecting the Three who are God, Thomas Aquinas, recognizing only two purely spiritual faculties – intellect and will – in us, saw their 'movements' of knowledge and love as reflecting the coming of the Word and the coming of the Spirit from the Father. He took from Augustine the idea of a 'word of the heart', a concept that is formed within the mind and is then expressed outwardly by means of a spoken word. When I form a concept, this understanding is both from my mind and within my mind. This is a poor analogy for how it is with God: the Word is both from the Father and yet is not outside the divine Being.

Besides knowing things outside me, I can come to know myself. Since I am human, this knowledge is partial and is built up slowly. But by reflection on myself I can achieve some understanding of what I am. This understanding is derived from myself yet remains within myself, until I express myself to others. We can picture the Father knowing Himself fully and perfectly, and expressing the whole of what He is in His Word, His perfect Image. This is not a process in time, it is not the creation of something outside God. The unity between Father and Word is beyond the imagination of us who are so complex and who develop over time. All the same, having come to some knowledge, I can rest for a time pondering the truth I have arrived at, and enjoying its beauty; and this is a poor image for how, in God, the Father and the Word rest in each other in Their timeless life. We may then picture the Father expressing Himself to us by sending His Word to dwell among us in the flesh.

If the Son is the perfect self-expression of the Father, as the divine Word and Wisdom, then it is in Him that the Father expresses His plan of creation and salvation. He is like the craftsman's or artist's conception of the work he is to fashion. So the beauty of the divine Word is reflected by the vast array of galaxies throughout the universe, by the symmetry of crystals, by the delicate structures of living things, and by our human power to learn and to create. The Word in whom all this was planned, and through whom it was made, entered our world to light it up by His presence and to complete the divine plan by showing us the Father. In this world He showed us the Father by opening His arms on the cross; in the next it will be by opening to us the divine Being He has from the Father.

THE HOLY SPIRIT, DIVINE LOVE OF THE FATHER AND THE SON

Before his Passover,[7] Jesus announced the sending of 'another Paraclete' (Advocate), the Holy Spirit. At work since creation, having previously 'spoken through the prophets', the Spirit will now be with and in the disciples, to teach them . . . The Holy Spirit is thus revealed as another divine person with Jesus and the Father. The eternal origin of the Holy Spirit is revealed in his mission in time. The Spirit is sent to the apostles and to the Church both by the Father in the name of the Son, and by the Son in person, once he had returned to the Father. The sending of the Person of the Spirit after Jesus' glorification reveals in its fullness the mystery of the Holy Trinity.

(Catechism 243–244)

The Old Testament speaks of the Word, the Wisdom and the Name of God, in order to express the presence and action in the world of the God whom the world cannot contain. It also speaks of the *Spirit* of God. The other terms usually refer to God's action outside us, in creation, in history, in giving the Law, and to His presence in the Temple; most often, 'the Spirit of the Lord' is used when it is a case of God's presence within the human being. When God gives life to human beings (and the other animals), when He gives people the gifts of leadership or prophecy, and when He converts people to goodness, we frequently read of the Spirit being given, or of the Spirit doing these things:

I will put my Spirit within you, and you shall live.

(Ezekiel 37:14)

The Lord raised up . . . Othniel . . . The Spirit of the Lord
came upon him, and he judged Israel; he went out to war.

(Judges 3:10)

A new heart I will give you, and a new spirit I will put within you
. . . and I will put my Spirit within you, and cause you to walk in
my statutes.

(Ezekiel 36:26–27)

The Spirit is not a creature, for all these gifts are divine works,
not the work of a creature. Since they do not exhaust the power
or the holiness of God, the Bible preserves a sense of the
hiddenness of the God whose works partially reveal Him by this
literary device of 'the Spirit of the Lord'.

We have seen that concepts such as 'the Word' are applied to
Jesus in the New Testament. Given their meaning in the Old
Testament, they imply that Jesus, who is a man people could
see, hear and touch, is also God among us, revealed yet still
mysterious. The concept of the Spirit of the Lord is not applied
to Jesus. On the contrary, He promised to send us the Spirit,
and after His death and Resurrection the Spirit came upon His
followers to give them new strength and courage, helping them
preach, and live by, His message. On the evening after He rose
from the dead, Jesus breathed upon His disciples, saying
'Receive the Holy Spirit' (John 20:22). Fifty days later, on the
Jewish feast of Pentecost, many disciples were gathered
together, when they heard the rushing of a mighty wind and saw
tongues of fire resting on each of them. They were filled with
the Holy Spirit and became able to speak about God's mighty
works in various languages (Acts 2:2–4).

The New Testament sees the Spirit as responsible for the
same kind of gifts the Old Testament attributes to Him, but
gives us the sense of a richer outpouring of the Spirit than
happened in previous ages.

Now there are varieties of gifts, but the same Spirit . . . To each
is given the manifestation of the Spirit for the common good. To
one is given through the Spirit the utterance of wisdom . . . to
another the working of miracles, to another prophecy . . . All

these are inspired by one and the same Spirit, who apportions to each one individually as He wills.

(1 Corinthians 12:4–11)

In the light of what the Old Testament says about 'the Spirit', we can see that the New Testament is claiming that the Spirit who moves the hearts of Jesus' followers is 'God within us', revealed by His works yet still beyond our comprehension. The New Testament authors did not need to say explicitly 'The Spirit is God'. That was something they could take for granted. St Paul is happy to place the Spirit's dwelling in us in poetic parallel with our being the Temple of God:

Do you not know that you are God's Temple, and that God's Spirit dwells in you?

(1 Corinthians 3:16)

The Holy Spirit is not an impersonal force, but a divine Person, whose godhead can be seen if we explore Old Testament usage, and whose relationship with the Father and the Son is revealed in the New Testament. In John 14 – 16, talking to His disciples the night before He died, Jesus speaks of the Spirit as 'another Counsellor'.[8] He says that the Father will send the Spirit in His name, and that He Himself will send them the Spirit from the Father. This will be possible only because of His 'going away', that is, His death and rising to a new life not of this world.

Because the Son, the Word, is from the Father, He could be sent by the Father to be God-with-us. Because the Spirit is from the Father and the Son, They can send Him to be God-within-us. Any coming of the Spirit, but above all His special coming at Pentecost, is a kind of extension into this world of that relationship within the changeless life of God, in which the Spirit is from the Father and the Son, while remaining fully one with Them.

We saw that St Augustine claimed that the coming of the Spirit from the Son as well as from the Father was revealed to us by the way in which the Son gave the Spirit to His disciples. The Roman Catholic Church came to say in the Nicene Creed (the form recited at Mass) that the Spirit proceeds from the Father *and the Son*. The Eastern Orthodox Churches consider that we made that addition to the Creed without adequate authority. The Roman Catholic Church claims that the addition of 'and from the Son' has the sanction of long usage, papal approval and an Ecumenical Council, that of Florence (1439–45), to which some Eastern patriarchs came and at which the others were represented.

The Eastern Churches prefer to speak of the Spirit coming from the Father *through* the Son, and Western theologians have been happy to use that expression because the Son receives the whole divine Being from the Father, and with it He receives the personal characteristic of being the Source of the Holy Spirit.

Of all the gifts the Spirit gives, the noblest is love, as St Paul tells us (1 Corinthians 12:31 – 13:13). Therefore just as the coming to be of knowledge within the human mind served St Thomas Aquinas as an image for the 'coming' of the Word from the Father, so the coming to be of love within the human mind served him as an image for the 'coming' of the Spirit from the Father and the Son. For once I know something, I can love it. A kind of impetus arises within my mind towards what I love, which in some ways matches what I love. To put it crudely, when I come to know and love chocolate cake, a 'chocolate cake-shaped concept' and a 'chocolate cake-shaped impulse' arise within my mind. Both are *from* my mind and *within* my mind. By seeing the movement of love within our mind as a poor image for the coming of the Spirit within God, St Thomas was able to claim that it is not nonsensical to speak of the Spirit being from the Father and the Son, but not in the manner of a creature formed outside the divine nature.

The Hebrew, Greek and Latin words sometimes translated as 'spirit' can also mean 'breath' or 'wind'. This allowed St Thomas to suggest that the name, 'Spirit', is appropriate for the one who proceeds from the Father and the Son, because we can picture His coming as a kind of mental impulse, and breath and wind are the most ethereal impulses in our experience of the material world.

If we can picture the Father as expressing Himself fully in His Son, His Word, His perfect Image, we can also picture the Father and the Son rejoicing in each other, in such a way that Their mutual love comes forth as a distinct Person. It is difficult, when speaking of the Spirit as the Love and Joy of the Father and the Son, to create much sense of His personal status. A similar difficulty is felt in Western Christian art: when the Father is shown holding His crucified Son in His arms, the

Spirit is shown as a dove hovering between Them. This reminds us that just as the Word's sonship is shown in His death on the cross, so the Spirit's role is shown us by His appearance as a dove of reconciliation and peace at Jesus' Baptism, and by the wind and fire of the Pentecost experience. But dove, wind and fire do not seem as personal as the third angel of the Eastern icon of the Trinity. We must remember, of course, that the divine Persons are not just larger versions of human persons. To picture Father and Son in too personal a way can be as misleading as to picture the Spirit in too impersonal a way.

Having said 'The Son proceeds as the Word in a manner [mirrored in the] intellect; but the Holy Spirit [proceeds] as Love in a manner [mirrored in the] will', St Thomas adds 'By the Holy Spirit the Father loves not only the Son but Himself and us as well' (*Summa*, I, 36.2 and 37.2 ad 3). Just as God's creative and saving work is planned in the divine Word, so His creative and saving purpose is formed in the divine Love, the Holy Spirit. The Father's love for all His creatures is there in the eternal life of God, in the Person of the Holy Spirit, who is manifest in the care God shows for all His creatures, and especially in the vitality of all living things. The Spirit is reflected more wonderfully still by the power of love found in human beings. Since God has an extra special love for all those He invites into His friendship, the crowning work of the Spirit is to dwell in our hearts to draw us into the life of the Holy Trinity. He makes us reflect Himself, to be guided by the Love that He is – and this means that we are to imitate the self-giving love of Jesus, in whom the Spirit was at work with unparalleled power.

NOTES

1 *Against the Arians* III, 4, translated in *The Early Christian Fathers*, ed. Henry Bettenson (OUP, Oxford, 1956), p. 395.

2 Henry Bettenson, *The Later Christian Fathers* (OUP, Oxford, 1972), p. 119.

3 Translation by Mark Musa (Penguin Classics, 1986), vol, III, p. 393.

4 In classical Hebrew, vowels were not written. By the time vowel-signs came to be used, the divine Name was not pronounced by the Jews.

5 The implication is not that the Jewish race, or even that the Jewish

people of the time, killed Jesus. 'The Jews' refers to the authorities in Jerusalem, rather as we might say, 'The French declared war', when we mean that the authorities in Paris did so. If the term 'the Jews' did refer to all those of Jewish race, it would include Jesus Himself, His Mother, His closest followers and those of His relatives who became important Christian leaders!

6 Sometimes He is shown on the cross, with the Father holding the arms of the cross. Sometimes He is shown slain, held against His Father's breast. The fact that an Old Testament image is used for the Father does not imply that we know of His fatherhood except through Jesus' sonship.

7 The Passover (*pesah* in Hebrew, *pascha* in Greek) is the Jewish feast celebrating the deliverance from Egypt under Moses (see Exodus 12 – 14). That deliverance, and the ritual commemorating it, were prophetic of Jesus' liberating death and Resurrection, which can therefore be referred to as His 'Passover' or 'Paschal Mystery'.

8 The Greek word *paraklētos* might be rendered as 'advocate', 'helper', 'friend', 'counsellor', 'comforter', 'defender'.

CHAPTER 3

ABIDING IN THE FATHER

OUR GOAL IS TO KNOW GOD

God put us in the world to know, to love, and to serve him, and so to come to Paradise. Beatitude[1] makes us 'partakers of the divine nature' [2 Peter 1:4] and of eternal life . . . this communion of life and love with the Trinity, with the Virgin Mary, the angels and all the blessed, is called 'heaven'. Heaven is the ultimate end and fulfilment of the deepest human longings, the state of supreme, definitive happiness . . . . Such beatitude surpasses the understanding and powers of man. It comes from an entirely free gift of God: whence it is called supernatural, as is the grace that disposes man to enter into the divine joy.

(*Catechism* 1721, 1024, 1722)

IN making us like Himself, God has made us for Himself. Only in communion with the Holy Trinity, our Maker, can we come to perfect fulfilment, to full and lasting joy. The image of God that we are realizes its dignity when it is so close to God as to reflect His glory as brightly as it can. This state of glory for which we hope is called *Heaven*.

St Thomas saw the human power to know as a reflection of the divine Wisdom, who comes from the Father as His Word, His self-expression. Our power to love is an image of the Spirit, who comes from the Father and the Son as Their Love and Joy. Because of these powers, we are open to the true and the good, and while we can rejoice in the goodness of the things and people around us, we can also search for new truths and new forms of goodness. Our thirst is to be fully satisfied by knowing *the* Truth, God Himself, and by enjoying *the* Good, God Himself. In Him, we shall value our fellow creatures more, not less.

But can the human mind really know God? We saw in Chapter I that we can say what God is not, and that when we say such things as 'God is love', we speak literally but do not know what we mean, since we cannot fathom the depths of God's love. We have power to know the things around us, a power given us by the creative Word – for rather as the Sun energizes the world of nature, and lights up its beauty for us to see, so the Word holds all things in being, and gives strength to our minds that we may grasp the patterns He has put into them. But our eyes cannot gaze directly on the Sun. How much more does the divine beauty defeat our feeble minds. From the things around us we draw images of God, but the image is not the reality. All our ideas are a kind of structuring of our mind, and because the structures of our mind are limited, they are in proportion to the limited structures in the things we know. They cannot be in proportion to the unlimited God.

Are we then to be frustrated? Is our openness to the true and the good never to be satisfied by communion with the divine source of truth and goodness? If our eyes were strengthened we could see the Sun, and because it shines with its own light it would not have to be lit up for us to see it. If our minds were strengthened we could know God, and because He is the truth we would not need to have inadequate ideas about Him, we could have *Him* in our minds. This is what we hope for, this is what Heaven consists in: God will give new strength to our minds, that He may give Himself to our minds and we may receive the divine Guest. Already dwelling within us as our Creator, He will dwell within us as our Friend whose company we can endure without being overwhelmed. This is called the *beatific vision*, the knowledge of God that brings us perfect bliss.

Some theologians have seen Heaven as a continuing voyage into God. St Thomas saw it as a resting in God. We must actually come to know *what* God is, incredible though this sounds. It does not follow that we will exhaust the divine depths in this knowledge, rather as a professor of zoology may know what 'animal' means, but will not be able to see in one glance all the different patterns of animal life which there are and which there might have been if evolution had taken a different course. We will not be able to see in God all the worlds He could have made, the full extent of His power. But we will come home to a knowledge of His nature. Even now, I can gaze on some work of art, or contemplate a new mathematical theorem, and lose track of time as I appreciate the beauty I am faced with. Heaven will not be year after year of learning fact after fact, but a timeless rejoicing in the unlimited Beauty. In Heaven, we will share God's own eternity.

The power to know God as He is, is a *supernatural* gift; it goes beyond the natural capacities of any creature, human or angelic. In giving us this gift, God will be lifting us up above our natural state, to His own level. Without ceasing to be creatures who depend on God for our very being, we shall be *divine*, for we shall share God's own knowledge of Himself, His bliss, His life. St Thomas says that we shall be *friends* of God, for friends have a certain equality, they share life, they enjoy each other's company. To say we are to be friends of the incomprehensible God is to make an amazing claim, and to point to a destiny quite different from the absorption into a state with no individuality some Eastern religions look for. The personalities of human friends are enriched by a relationship in which closeness does not conflict with cherishing the other. Our communion with God will be unimaginably enriching as He brings to share His happiness those He holds in being.

Closeness and otherness are found in a specially rich way in the Holy Trinity, where the Three are distinct and perfectly one. It is in fact in Their relationships that we are to share in Heaven! Our power to know, which is a sharing in the divine Wisdom, will be fulfilled when that Wisdom dwells in our minds to show us the Father. He is the self-expression, the Word or utterance of the Father; it is His role in the life of the Trinity to express perfectly what the Father is. In the beatific vision, the Word will enlarge our minds so that through Him the Father can be known. Therefore in Matthew 11:27 Jesus says, 'No one knows the Son except the Father, and no one knows the Father except the Son and any one to whom the Son chooses to reveal Him'. We are not promised a share in the Father's knowledge of the Son; we are offered a share in the Son's knowledge of the Father.

If the Word is to be in us, we also are to be in Him. St John tells us that the only Son 'is in the bosom of the Father' (John 1:18). He records how Jesus prayed to His Father that those 'whom Thou hast given me, may be with me where I am' (17:24). We are to abide with the Son in the bosom of the

Father; we are to share in His sonship, in His closeness to the Father; with Him, we are to gaze on the Father, knowing the divine nature in its Source. We are to be *children of God*, sharing the glory of the divine Son. So John says 'To all who received Him . . . He gave power to become children of God' (John 1:12).

The Father and the Son rejoice in each other, and the Spirit is Their mutual Love and Joy. If we are to share the Son's relationship with the Father, we are to share in Their Love and Joy. Our power to love, to rejoice in the good, which is a sharing in the Holy Spirit, will come to perfection in Heaven when the Spirit dwells in us most richly. He will enlarge our wills so that we can respond to the Father's goodness with a love of supernatural intensity. The Spirit is sent to us while we are still in this world, to draw us into the relationship of love between the Son and the Father. He makes us able to live even now as children of the Father, so that we stand to inherit a share in the Son's glory; He makes our earthly lives into a journey towards the Father. As the bond of love between the Father and the Son, it is His role to draw us to the Father whom we love as His children, and unite us to Him eternally.

So the Son and the Spirit were sent by the Father to carry out the work of *salvation*. The Greek and Hebrew words we translate as 'save' or 'salvation' are basically to do with rescue. But the Latin word *salus* conveniently means both 'rescue' and 'well-being', and while it is true that we need to be set free from what holds us back from God, our great and wonderful hope is to enjoy the well-being which is a share in God's own bliss, an abiding with the Son in the Father, filled with Their Joy.

OUR GOAL IS THE 'CITY' AND 'KINGDOM OF GOD'

We firmly believe, and hence we hope that, just as Christ is truly risen from the dead and lives for ever, so after death the righteous will live for ever with the risen Christ and he will raise them up on the last day . . . At the end of time, the Kingdom of God will come in its fullness. After the universal judgement, the righteous will reign for ever with Christ, glorified in body and soul. The universe itself will be renewed . . . this consummation

will be the final realization of the unity of the human race . . .
The beatific vision . . . will be the ever-flowing well-spring of
happiness, peace, and mutual communion.

(Catechism 989, 1042, 1045)

There are other aspects to the glory we hope for besides
knowing the Father as His children. If one soul only were to rest
in God, she would be perfectly happy. But God's plan is to save
the human race, not just one individual, to save human beings,
not just human souls. Therefore our Christian hope is for the
resurrection of the body. The souls of those who die as God's
friends can enjoy the beatific vision, since the faculties of
intellect and will do not in themselves require a bodily organ.
But our journey's goal is not reached while only our souls are in
bliss, for a soul is not a human being. In the final resurrection
God will restore us to wholeness, and of that the Resurrection of
Jesus Christ is the pledge. Then the whole company of the saved
will rejoice together, complete.

The hope for a final resurrection appeared among the Jews
before the coming of Jesus Christ, but not all Jews then shared
it. Jesus taught that there would be a final resurrection, and in
St John's Gospel we read of His own role in it:

The hour is coming when all who are in the tombs will hear his
[the Son of God's] voice and come forth, those who have done
good, to the resurrection of life, and those who have done evil, to
the resurrection of judgement . . . This is the will of my Father,
that every one who sees the Son and believes in him should have
eternal life; and I will raise him up at the last day.

(5:28–29, 6:40)

The Jewish custom of burying the dead was adopted by the
Christian Church, and the Catholic Church still prefers burial
to cremation because burial speaks more eloquently of resting
in the hope of rising again. The early Christians preserved and
venerated the remains of the martyrs who allowed themselves to
be put to death rather than renounce their belief in Jesus and
abandon the hope they had in Him, and this veneration was
extended to the relics of other saints whose bodies had clearly
been temples of the Holy Spirit, given that their lives bore
powerful witness to God's love.

However, we must not suppose that cremation, or the total
decay of a dead person's body, places any difficulty in the way of

the final resurrection. In the course of our earthly lives, the actual matter in our bodies is in flux, but each of us remains a single organism because what we absorb from our food and drink is incorporated into the living structure that persists. If it is the immortal soul that forms the body, i.e. is (partly) expressed in that continuing living structure, then at the resurrection it will be possible for the soul that has survived to incorporate even totally new matter into the risen body. This is different from reincarnation: in reincarnation, a soul inhabits one body after another, but in the resurrection the soul is made able once more to form its own, characteristic body.

We cannot imagine what the risen body will be like. St Paul implies that it will differ from our present state as a plant differs from the seed it grows out of (see 1 Corinthians 15:35–44). One way of expressing the risen state is to say that the bliss of God's presence in the mind that knows Him, will 'overflow' into bliss and glory for the whole of our being, for all our faculties and for our bodily condition. So, though its state will be very different from its present condition, the risen body will be more, not less, human. As humans, we communicate through our bodies, but with some difficulty; the risen body will be, as it were, transparent to the spiritual reality of our friendship with God. Therefore it can be called 'a spiritual body'. It will participate in its own way in the soul's sharing in God's eternity, so it will not be subject to the laws that govern the behaviour of matter in this universe.

Nor can we set out any programme for the future resurrection. We know no date for what Jesus calls 'the last day' in the quotation above. The Scriptures give us many images for what is certainly a future transformation of the order of the world, but no straightforward description. The important thing is for us to live now as those who look forward in hope to a salvation that God has begun in Jesus' Resurrection and reveals in symbolic form in the Scriptures and the sacraments. If we knew the precise date for the end, we would not live in constant hope, but would put off our being ready. Whatever will happen in the final refashioning of the world will be the fulfilment of the whole material creation. That can be said, even if the only material things to be glorified are the bodies of God's friends. They will be glorified on behalf of the universe that was their home. The use of material elements in the sacraments is a sign that God will, somehow, bring the material creation to a glorious fulfilment.

The social dimension of human nature is most important. Therefore the resurrection world is pictured in Scripture as a feast and as a city. In St Matthew's Gospel we hear of 'the Kingdom of Heaven'; in St Mark's and St Luke's Gospels we hear of 'the Kingdom of God'. Both phrases really mean 'the rule of God'. But we can use the term, *the Kingdom*, to refer to that state, that human-and-divine community, in which all the forces that obscure or spoil God's work are overcome, and He is perfectly known, loved and adored. In it, we shall be in communion both with God, and with each other, and our common rejoicing will add to our bliss. There will be degrees of glory in the Kingdom, depending not upon our visible importance on earth, but on the love with which we have journeyed into God. Not all shall know God with equal intensity.[2] But so great will our love be, that there will be no room for envy, only a greater thanksgiving as we delight in what God has given to others as if it were given to ourselves.

OUR GOAL LIGHTS UP OUR PILGRIMAGE

The promised restoration which we are awaiting has already begun in Christ, is carried forward in the mission of the Holy Spirit, and through Him continues in the Church. There we learn through faith the meaning, too, of our temporal life, as we perform, with hope of good things to come, the task committed to us in this world by the Father, and work out our salvation (cf. Philippians 2:12) . . . [Christ] arouses not only a desire for the age to come, but, by that very fact, He animates, purifies and strengthens those noble longings too by which the human family strives to make its life more human.

(Vatican II, *Dogmatic Constitution on the Church*, vii, 48;
Pastoral Constitution on the Church in the Modern World, iii, 38)[3]

Our life in this world is a journey to the Father. It can well be called a 'pilgrimage'. The Second Vatican Council saw the Christian Church as a pilgrim people, on our way to God's Kingdom. A pilgrimage is a journey to a holy place, and often the journey itself involves happiness and hardship, which lend a precious quality to the joy of arrival. Our journey to God involves the joys and trials of this life, which are valuable now, and contribute to our eternal thanksgiving. We are not meant to despise this life because it is a journey. Vatican II did not simply try to *balance* our concern for this world and our concern for the world to come; the quotations above say that the hope of heaven should *animate and purify* our attempts to cherish humanity.

The New Testament is marked with an eager longing for the return of Christ in glory to bring about the resurrection of the dead, that is, to share His own risen glory with those who belong to Him. Almost its last words are 'Come, Lord Jesus!' But we are not taught to sit back and do nothing as we wait for a better world, we are told to watch at all times, since we do not know when the Master is to come. He must find us 'at our post' (Mark 13:32–37). The hope for 'new heavens and a new earth where justice dwells' is meant to make us consider 'what sort of persons ought [we] to be' (2 Peter 3:11) here and now. We must, in brief, cherish justice now, if we are to enjoy it eternally. We must live by the values of the Kingdom we hope to enter, in order to lay claim to it and be ready for it.

We can put this by saying that we have to live as God's children in this world if we hope to live as His children in the next. If we hope to share His life and reflect His glory, we must begin now by sharing His love and reflecting His care. We must minister God's goodness to those around us, in imitation of Jesus Christ, if we are to receive what His goodness has in store for us. In fact, since the best picture we now have of the sonship of the divine Word is His death on a cross, we must be prepared in some way to share His cross if we want to share his sonship. Only by the Holy Spirit's help can we do this; it is His job to make us into our Father's children. His power can be at work even when the human contribution is feeble or lacking: an infant who is baptized, or someone who comes to faith in God on his deathbed, may not be able to perform any action that reflects God's care for the people around, but a share in the divine life is still planted in them, able to grow into the life of glory.

The question can be asked, 'Why did God not give us Heaven straight away?' All sorts of worlds could have been made by

God, each with its own beauty. But part of the beauty of this world, a world of pilgrimage, is that Heaven is both *gift* and *reward*. For the sake of our greater glory, God makes us able to direct our lives towards Him. By our deliberate choice, by deeds of love, we can *merit* life with God. We can make a contribution to our final joy. Bear in mind, however, that we can only do anything worthy of eternal life because the Holy Spirit Himself inspires and makes possible our good works. In crowning the saints' merits, God is crowning His own gifts. The glory of Heaven is cause for thanksgiving rather than pride. Remember also that heaven is not a commodity to be bought; it is life with God. Therefore when we consider a Christian's good works, we do not need to ask, 'Are they done for her sake, or for God's?' God is neither employer nor beneficiary, but Friend. Now when human friends do things together, or for each other, what they do is done for both their sakes. Their lives are bound together and the good of either is experienced as the good of both. The drive towards fulfilment that is in each by nature, becomes a concern for the fulfilment of the two. If, then, we love God as our Friend, we want to live with Him and share His joy, while it is His delight that this should happen. What our love for God inspires us to do, is done for our fulfilment and God's glory, at one and the same time. And to want God's glory is to want our own glory, for God cannot be made more glorious in Himself; He is glorified by His creatures coming to reflect His glory more brightly.

The particular beauty of human life includes not just the kind of growth found among the other animals, but the use of reason to plan for freely-chosen goals and the satisfaction achieved by completing our projects. God draws us towards Himself in a way that suits the nature He Himself has given us, making us able to choose Him as our goal and to live for that goal.

The resurrection of the body in which we have served God and others will be God's affirmation of our life-story. The relationships we build up now will be preserved within the community of the Kingdom. We view our present life wrongly if, in the light of Heaven, we treat it as of no value at all; or if we cling frantically to pleasures that are only meant to be transitory; or if we suppose that this life is our only life, a journey into nothingness and not into light.

NOTES

1 i.e. the final, all-fulfilling state of bliss and happiness to which it is God's loving purpose to bring us.
2 A student and a professor of zoology both know what 'an animal' is, but the professor has the more profound and extensive knowledge of that concept. In a roughly analogous way, all who are in Heaven know what God is, yet some fathom Him more deeply, and none fully.
3 *The Documents of Vatican II*, translated by Walter M. Abbott (Geoffrey Chapman, London, 1967).

PART 2

THE SPIRIT GUIDES OUR PILGRIMAGE

In Part 2 we consider how the Holy Spirit makes our life into a pilgrimage to the Father. First, we turn to the gifts He gives us, of which the greatest is a share in the divine life, and we look at ways in which this life flourishes and grows. Then, in Chapter 5, we examine the difficulties that have to be overcome on our way to the Father, particularly the sin that has to be forgiven. This provides an opportunity to discuss the problem of evil.

CHAPTER 4

THE LIFE OF GRACE

SHARING IN THE LIFE OF THE HOLY TRINITY

Grace is *favour*, the *free and undeserved help* that God gives us to
respond to his call to become children of God . . . Grace is a
participation in the life of God. It introduces us into the intimacy
of Trinitarian life . . . as an 'adopted son' [the Christian] can
. . . call God 'Father', in union with the only Son . . . This
vocation to eternal life is *supernatural*. It depends entirely on
God's gratuitous initiative, for he alone can reveal and give
himself . . . Sanctifying grace . . . perfects the soul itself to
enable it to live with God, to act by his love.

(*Catechism* 1996–1998, 2000)

S PEAKING of our hope for life with God, 2 Peter 1:3–4 says
that we have been called to God's 'own glory and excellence', and that we are made able to 'become partakers of the
divine nature'. We have seen that our share in God's life will be
a sharing in the sonship of the divine Word, a sharing of His
relationship with the Father. But 1 John 3:1–2 exclaims: 'See
what love the Father has given us, that we should be called
children of God; and so we are . . . Beloved, *we are God's
children now*; it does not yet appear what we shall be . . . ' We
can become children of the Father while still in this world; we
are offered here and now a share in God's life, a share that can
blossom forth into glory in the world to come. As has been said,
it is by living as God's children that we can lay hold on eternal
life with our Father.

In Romans 8:14–17, St Paul says that those 'who are led by
the Spirit of God are sons of God', and speaks of how we are
'fellow heirs with Christ'. We can say, then, that the Holy Spirit
draws those who receive Him into the relationship between Son

69

and Father, so that by bestowing His Spirit on people the Father adopts them as His children in Jesus Christ. We can live even now within the Holy Trinity!

The Fathers of the Church spoke of how Christians are *divinized*. In later centuries our sharing in the life of the Holy Trinity came to be called *sanctifying grace*. The Latin word *gratia* can mean 'thanks'; it can also refer to someone's goodwill or favour, so it can be used of God's special love by which He invites us to share His own joy. In the present context 'grace' means a *gift* which God gives us in His love, the gift of a share in His life which sanctifies us, that is, makes us holy by uniting us with God. God as it were takes hold of what we are, transforming it, raising it, so that we live on a new level, while we do not cease to be human. St Thomas likes to say that 'grace builds on nature'; it enriches and deepens what God has already given us as our Creator, rather than bypassing it.

God's greatest work is to grace us with a share in His own life. When the universe sprang into being something great was accomplished. When this world ends, and the life of grace grows into the life of glory, God's power will be made visible, as we reflect His brightness. But when a baby is baptized, or when someone who has turned from God comes back to God, something still greater takes place! From being a mere creature, the person receiving grace becomes a child and a friend of God, *becomes divine*. Except for dramatic conversions like St Paul's, this work of God is not a miracle, since it does not strike us with wonder. It is not a miracle for another reason: it fulfils an openness to Himself that God has put into us by making us in His own image. But it is more wonderful than a miracle, for there is no greater disproportion than that between the creature and a child of God.

Being a child of God is something truly *supernatural*. It is beyond the power of any creature to lay hold on the life of God; He alone can lift us up to that inexpressible dignity. But the supernatural is not at all the same as the spectacular or the spooky.[1] 'It does not yet appear what we shall be'; we do not enjoy the vision of God, or shine with glory, or experience Heaven. Many people do have 'religious experiences'. Some of these are products of their own psychology or of suggestion; some are the work of God reminding us of our thirst for Him.[2] Even if we enjoy experiences from God it does not follow that we are holy. We can resist God's call. Some saints – not all – have had striking mystical experiences. They have not relied on them, indeed some have grown closest to God in a 'dark night of the soul' in which all sweetness was withdrawn from them. Very rarely has a saint had a fleeting glimpse of the beatific vision itself. It *is* important for us to show that we share God's life, in fact we must do this by performing divine actions! But the kind of actions that count as divine are such things as saying the prayer 'Our Father', forgiving our enemies, enduring suffering for the sake of justice, and caring for those in need because we share God's concern for them.

> When we cry, 'Abba! Father!' it is the Spirit Himself bearing witness with our spirit that we are children of God . . . fellow heirs with Christ, provided we suffer with Him in order that we may also be glorified with Him.
>
> (Romans 8:15–17)
>
> Love your enemies and pray for those who persecute you, so that you may be sons of your Father who is in Heaven.
>
> (Matthew 5:44–45)

The divinity of such actions is only visible if we have eyes of faith to see it!

Clearly we depend on God for the life of grace, even as we depend on Him for human life. Only God can make us divine. Once we have grace in us, we can do what merits eternal life – though not without God's continual help. God's life in us has a power to grow and to issue in glory. But when it first comes, and when it is restored after we have lost it, God's life is totally a gift, even though, under God's guidance, it often comes in the course of what may seem a very human process. Christian parents bring their baby to be baptized. A non-Christian is impressed by a Christian he meets, and wants to share the faith that inspires her. Someone who has turned from God experiences remorse and is encouraged by a friend to confess the sin and perform a gesture of sorrow. God is at work in the depths of these processes, even as the grace He gives will be at work in the depths of the Christian behaviour it makes possible.

FAITH, HOPE AND CHARITY

A virtue is an habitual and firm disposition to do the good. It allows the person not only to perform good acts, but to give the

best of himself . . . The theological virtues . . . are infused by
God into the souls of the faithful to make them capable of acting
as his children and of meriting eternal life . . . Faith is first of all
a personal adherence of man to God. At the same time, and
inseparably, it is a *free assent to the whole truth that God has
revealed* . . . by [hope] we desire the Kingdom of Heaven and
eternal life as our happiness, placing our trust in Christ's
promises and relying not on our own strength, but on the help of
the grace of the Holy Spirit . . . by [charity] we love God above
all things for his own sake, and our neighbour as ourselves for
the love of God.

(Catechism 1803, 1813, 150, 1817, 1822)

What something is, its nature, expresses or deploys itself in
what it can do, its faculties. Our human nature is shown by the
particular range of faculties we possess. The faculties something has allow it to perform activities that are meant to lead to
the kind of well-being that suits it. The well-being or fulfilment
that suits human nature is achieved in the harmonious balance
of the many activities that are part of a healthy human life.

Many of our faculties are quite subtle, and can be channelled
towards different uses. I can structure my intellect with the
concepts of chemistry, and so use it easily and enjoyably to
understand chemical reactions; or I can structure it with the
concepts of music, and so become able to appreciate better the
works of great composers. Not just my intellect, but also my
will and emotions, can be moulded and adapted by 'habits' to
make certain kinds of action easier, to make me able to perform
them by a kind of 'second nature'. This kind of habit is different
from a nervous tic that I may not like but cannot break; as I
develop over the years I build up a body of habits, of skills,
attitudes, reactions and so on, that express what I have tried to
make of myself, that embody my values and preferences.

Habits can be life-enhancing, and then they are called *virtues*.
The Latin word *virtus* means 'strength', and a virtue is a kind of
strength of character; it means that 'by second nature', readily
and enjoyably, I react and behave in a way that leads towards
human fulfilment. By contrast, a *vice* is a settled way of acting
that militates against human flourishing. It is different from
'moral weakness'. To take a fairly trivial example: if I am given
a box of chocolates, because I am morally weak I will find it

difficult to decide whether to eat them all myself or to share them. If I were virtuous, I would find delight in sharing them, and do so automatically – but still freely, because in sharing them I would express the kind of person I had made of myself and was happy to be. If on the other hand I were vicious, I would find delight in eating all the chocolates myself – but it would be a false, illusory delight, because the greed and meanness I had built up would cramp my personality and cut off the greater joy of sharing.

Now what we are, our nature, is lifted to a new level when God gives us His grace and makes us live in a divine way, as His children. It is fitting that this divine life should express or deploy itself in divine virtues, in God-given strengths that mould and adapt our faculties so that they can be used in a divine way. That is to say, God gives us the resources to live in the way that suits our status as His children, to do what leads to the fulfilment and joy we ought to inherit as fellow-heirs with Christ. By a kind of second nature we react and behave in a divine way that leads to a certain joy and peace now, and in the end to the bliss of God's Kingdom.

Of the strengths that God gives, the three most important are *faith, hope and charity*. These are traditionally called the *theological virtues*, that is, strengths that come from God and lead us to Him. Faith makes us able to recognize God's offer of eternal life, and the means He supplies to help us towards that goal. Hope is a kind of divine enthusiasm that makes possible the effort of the Christian life. Charity is that friendship with God which makes Him the goal of our lives, the love that joins us to Him and draws us towards Him.

In human affairs we *know* the things we can prove for ourselves, and we hazard *opinions* when we are uncertain. But we also *believe* things on the authority of those we trust. An engineer who is not good at physics will accept formulae from the physicist; in marriage, the bride and groom must accept each other's promise of loyalty. Now no one can prove that God is the Holy Trinity, or that we are made able to share the life of the Holy Trinity because Jesus was crucified outside Jerusalem 2,000 years ago. These are truths that God knows – as do the saints and angels who already gaze into Him – and which we must *believe* on His authority. *Faith* is the gift of God that enables us to recognize the Father's self-revelation in Jesus

Christ His Son, a revelation handed down to us in the Scriptures and the Church's tradition. It gives us confidence because God is supremely trustworthy. We can use our reason in support of faith, by showing how beautifully God's plan of salvation fits our needs, by seeing how the different parts of our faith cohere, and by demonstrating that the difficulties put forward as objections to the Christian faith do not work. But the most brilliant theologian is as dependent on the gift of faith as the simplest believer.

Faith is 'a supernatural gift of God'; it is a God-given communion with God. We are joined to Him in trust, and we have an insight into His plan. But it is a gift for this life only, destined to be replaced by the clear knowledge of God. Therefore it comes to us in apparently human ways – recall the story of St Augustine's conversion – and its presence is manifest by such straightforward signs as saying the Creed and meaning what you say. It involves belonging to the company of Jesus' disciples, to the 'community of faith' which cherishes the Scriptures and teaches authentically what God has shown us. An attitude of credulity is not the same thing as faith; a determination to belong to the Catholic Church and accept her teaching is.

Sometimes in the Scriptures the word 'faith' stands for our total response to God's invitation, and in that sense it could not exist without a love for God and a sharing in His life. The narrower meaning explored in the paragraphs above, that is, our acceptance of the truth God has revealed, is drawn by St Thomas from Hebrews 11:1 and 6. In this sense, too, faith involves trust in God, but it is possible to believe the truths He has shown us and still disobey Him seriously: wicked Christians can be found. So the Letter of St James tells us that faith that does not issue in works of love is dead.

Hope, like faith, is also found in human life. We are often faced with worthwhile goals which it takes effort to achieve. Then we need to be spurred on by enthusiasm. A trivial example would be walkers wondering whether they can get to the next pub before it closes for the afternoon. If they think they can, they put a spurt on. But the Second Vatican Council declared that the Church shares in 'the joy and the hope, the sorrow and anxiety of the people of this age'. Since that Council met in the early 1960s new hopes have emerged on the basis of new technology, and we have become conscious of new problems that defy hope. It is right that Christian hope should pervade and ennoble – but also test and purify – human hopes both great and small. At depth, however, Christian hope is a God-given eagerness for the best possible goal, and has a certainty no creaturely difficulty can dampen. For we hope for the supreme joy of sharing God's own bliss – and that goal is not just difficult, it is impossible for a mere creature to attain. Our confidence rests upon God's power and the love He has shown us. In the strength of that reliance we pray to God, asking His help, and we make the effort to obey God's law. Whenever we turn from God in sin, we hope for forgiveness. So hope does not rely on human strength, nor does it presume upon some kind of 'duty' God has to save us. But it excludes any despair based on our weakness or our faults, for God has the power and the will to overcome even the obstacles I may place in the way of my growth towards Him.

In 1 Corinthians 13, St Paul tells us that the greatest gift of the Holy Spirit is *love*. The word 'love' is a very flexible word. I can say that I love chocolate, that a couple I know are in love, that I love God and that the Holy Spirit is the divine love. Our experience of loving God, of being loyal to Him, of letting our love for God inform our choices and actions, and so on, will not be a radically different experience from our human experience of love and loyalty, or of the occasional clash of loyalties. At the same time, we must bear in mind that the features of one kind of love need not apply to another. A long-married couple may not experience the emotional excitement of courtship, yet belong to each other very deeply, and the depth of their relationship may have been achieved through periods of faithfulness when the initial delight of marriage cooled off and temptations to infidelity had to be resisted. Our love for God must be a faith-fulness to Him, and may or may not include feelings of 'being in love'. In fact such feelings may sometimes blind us to a lack of love for God, which a look at our behaviour would reveal.

The usual word for love in the New Testament is *agapē*, which was rarely used in everyday Greek. Maybe the first Christians chose to use it so that they could speak about our love for God without pagan notions intruding. The Latin word used to translate *agapē* is *caritas*, which comes from the word *carus*, 'dear'. So *charity* should be a warm word: it means 'holding God dear, and holding other people dear because they are dear to

God'. From the eighteenth century the phrase 'cold as charity' begins to be found, perhaps because by then a lot of poor relief had been institutionalized and officials had to judge who deserved relief, and keep account of how funds were used. Before the monasteries were suppressed, and laws against begging passed, in the sixteenth century, the ideal of helping all who came asking, spontaneously and non-judgementally, would have been recognized if not always put into practice. So if we speak of Christian 'charity' we should avoid the overtone of coldness, and if we speak of Christian 'love' we should remember that this love is a matter of deeds and not just of feelings.

St Thomas defines 'charity' as a *friendship* with God. For we share something of our life and interests with our friends; so the love with which we are attracted to the God who has called us to share His life is truly a friendship. If I have a friend whose children are unpleasant I will still be concerned for them for my friend's sake; and if God is my friend I must share His interests and concerns, I must share His love and His care for those He loves and cares for, especially those He has given me the chance to care for. That includes myself! I must share God's love for myself, and do what helps me to grow and flourish as a child of God.

Thus it is a rare occurrence for the love of God to draw someone away from family ties and social commitments. More often, it enriches, confirms, deepens, purifies and enlarges our natural bonds. It makes us care for our families, friends, colleagues and fellow-citizens with a divine and no longer just a human love – and it makes us love those for whom we would have no merely human love: those distant from us and our enemies. Charity shares in God's power to overcome evil and work reconciliation: if we pay back evil with evil, we perpetuate enmity, but if we pay back evil with good we bring a new factor into the situation, which can transform it. We 'overcome evil with good' (Romans 12:21) and reveal ourselves as God's children (Matthew 5:45).

When he discusses the ways charity typically works, St Thomas gives special mention to almsgiving and fraternal correction. We show our Christian love by feeding the hungry, visiting prisoners, helping the sick, by hospitality or forgiveness, by educating the unlearned, by comforting the sorrowful and supporting others with our prayers, by helping and encouraging sinners mend their ways and return to God.

If we have grace, we have charity: if we have charity, we have grace. For the character of someone's life is determined by that person's priorities. We can live for power, or pleasure, or wealth . . . or for God. If we love God above all things, He becomes our 'top priority'. Our lives become 'God-shaped'. So the sign that we have God's life in us, the life of grace that is to grow into the life of glory, is that we love God above all things, and make Him our goal. This does not mean that we only do religious things day and night, or that we do nothing but perform works of charity. Someone who lives for power, with power as the goal that shapes his life, will do many things not directly geared to acquiring power. Our love for God and neighbour will certainly express itself in various ways, and it will hold us back from doing things contrary to love; but there are many pursuits we can engage in which are neither obligatory nor forbidden. However, charity brings new strength, purpose and integrity to the many other virtues we need, for it puts all the good that we do in the context of a life lived for God.

THE GIFTS AND GUIDANCE OF THE HOLY SPIRIT

. . . the more docile we are to the promptings of grace, the more we grow in inner freedom . . . By the working of grace, the Holy Spirit educates us in spiritual freedom in order to make us free collaborators in his work in the Church and in the world.

(Catechism 1742)

Charity is not just the greatest gift of the Holy Spirit, it is a kind of *sharing in* the Holy Spirit. It is a power of love that makes us like the divine Love Himself. Therefore when the Holy Spirit brings someone to grace, He is sent to that person by the Father and the Son. Faith and hope are to be replaced by knowledge and possession; in the Kingdom charity becomes stronger. Our love for God will grow when we enjoy His goodness and beauty; our sharing in the Holy Spirit of love will become a more intense sharing in the Holy Spirit of joy.

The Holy Spirit brings with Himself a variety of gifts and strengths. St Thomas points out that human reason can plan for the limited fulfilment human strength can achieve, but even when strengthened by faith it cannot plan adequately for the goal that is God's bliss. Faith is a kind of darkness as well as a kind of light. The Holy Spirit must prompt and guide us through the various circumstances of our Christian lives, and by His gifts must make us responsive to Him as a pupil must be attuned to the teacher's methods. The guidance of the Holy Spirit is not normally manifest in the form of 'inner voices'; such voices are often enough a form of delusion. Rather, when we ask God for guidance, read the Scriptures, listen to the Church and her Fathers and Doctors, take advice and think things through, the Spirit is at work in the depths of the process. We can resist His promptings; but the more we grow in love the more He will purify our ideas and impulses. Then we shall find ourselves more and more in tune with the Church's tradition and wisdom. If on the other hand we turn from God in serious sin we bring a fundamental flaw into our system of values and forfeit the Spirit's guidance

A great gift of the Holy Spirit is wisdom, the ability to make judgements in the light of the highest principles. Charity attaches us to God and makes life with Him our goal, and by wisdom we acquire a kind of 'divine perspective' on things, so that we see all reality as come from God, and evaluate everything according as it leads to Him or distracts from Him. As charity is a sharing in the Holy Spirit, so wisdom is a sharing in the divine Wisdom, the Son of God, who is sent to us from the Father when we come to grace.

Thus the life of grace involves the *indwelling* of the Holy Trinity. This is not just a matter of the Son and the Spirit making us to be like Them. God is present in all His creatures by acting on them. He is present in His friends in a quite new way, by *their response* to Him. God is in us as the known is in the knower and the beloved in the lover, when we are made able to believe in our Father and to begin to see things from His perspective, and to love Him as Friend.

The presence in us of the Holy Spirit, to whose guidance we are made responsive, is not at all a matter of 'being possessed'. Occasionally He does 'take people over', but if people are possessed, this is as a rule to be attributed to psychological disorder or evil spirits. The divine Spirit 'orders all things sweetly' (cf. Wisdom 8:1), and 'where the Spirit of the Lord is, there is freedom' (2 Corinthians 3:17). In Chapter 1, examining the diagram on page 17, we saw that God gives to His creatures 'structures and strengths' so that they can truly act out of their own power; now we note that when the Holy Spirit moulds our minds and hearts with various strengths, we are both totally dependent on Him and at the same time made able by Him to think and live rightly. He puts us in charge of our lives, so that we can direct them towards the fulfilment that is God, and enjoy now the fulfilment of living as human beings truly should. Therefore the Spirit brings freedom, integrity and humanity.

The diagram on page 17 showed the action of the gas on the water, and my choice to eat, as depending on God without being any the less the acts of the gas and of me. In a similar way, anything anyone does that leads towards life with God depends on God and is still that person's action. So we speak of *actual graces*, meaning that all those promptings of the Spirit, and all those thoughts, decisions and actions that promote our growth as God's children, are themselves gifts from the God who sets us free for Himself. One who does not yet have God's life in him is like someone still building up a human virtue by the effort of training: all that he does that carries him towards God's friendship is experienced with some surprise, since it is a God-given achievement beyond his previous capacity. Once sanctifying grace has been given and we are made divine, God's actual graces are the impulses that enable us to express our new nature as God's children.

The Spirit gives to some people skills or talents that they are meant to use in the service of the whole community: these can be called *charismatic gifts*. Or He may simply pick upon a particular person to perform a certain job, once or several times, without imparting a permanent facility. The tasks He enables people to perform include prophecy – in particular, the insight and skill with imagery that were involved in the composition of Scripture – preaching, teaching, and the working of miracles when these can help bring people to faith. St Paul criticizes the Christians of Corinth because they are using their spiritual gifts for self-aggrandizement and not in humble service, and so have focused on the more spectacular rather than the more useful gifts. He points out that these gifts have no automatic connection with the holiness, the degree of charity, of the person who has them. It is charity we must be most concerned to have; and when we have it, it will move us to use whatever other gifts we have for the good of others, in self-forgetfulness.

THE CHRISTIAN MORAL PROJECT

> Human virtues acquired by education, by deliberate acts and by a perseverance ever-renewed in repeated efforts are purified and elevated by divine grace. With God's help, they forge character and give facility in the practice of the good. The virtuous man is happy to practise them . . . *Prudence* is the virtue that disposes practical reason to discern our true good in every circumstance and to choose the right means of achieving it . . . *Justice* is the moral virtue that consists in the constant and firm will to give their due to God and neighbour . . . *Fortitude* is the moral virtue that ensures firmness in difficulties and constancy in the pursuit of the good . . . *Temperance* is the moral virtue that moderates the attraction of pleasures and provides balance in the use of created goods . . . Law is declared and established by reason as a participation in the providence of the living God . . . Conscience is a judgement of reason whereby the human person recognizes the moral quality of a concrete act that he is going to perform, is in the process of performing, or has already completed . . .
>
> (*Catechism* 1810, 1806–1809, 1951, 1778)

Some of the things that Christians do only make sense in the light of a belief in God and a hope for His Kingdom. When we meet together on Sunday to celebrate the Eucharist in memory of Jesus' death and Resurrection, we do something non-Christians do not do. When we fast from food or deny ourselves in other ways, in memory of Jesus' suffering, and when we pray to the Father in union with His Son, we make clear our Christian faith and hope. When people join religious orders, consecrating their lives to the service of God and of the Church in a special way, and stepping outside some of the structures of human society so as to be more free for prayer, or preaching, or other forms of service, they bear witness to God's call.

Many things done by Christians do make perfect human sense. They would be done by any human being of good-will and integrity, for they contribute to human fulfilment, and do not need to be justified by reference to a supernatural goal. The Christian moral project incorporates the human moral project, the pursuit of human well-being in which we can be one with our non-Christian fellow-citizens. All pursuit of the good can be part of the pilgrimage towards the unlimited Good. The Spirit, whose love deepens our natural bonds, brings moral health and wholeness to the various facets of our psyche and to our many relationships, making up for what is lacking in human strength. By His help and our effort we can grow in human virtue, so that our thoughts, reactions and behaviour come to suit our humanity and therefore our dignity as God's children. Thus we may flourish. The chief human virtues explored by many Christian theologians (who themselves drew on the great classical moralists) are *prudence*, or good moral sense; *justice*; *fortitude* or courage; and *temperance* or self-control.

Good sense moulds our power to think or reason, so that we can make wise decisions. It enables us to apply general moral principles to the situations we find ourselves in. We must exercise it in our own regard when, for example, we have to make an important decision about our job. We need to take advice from others and consider the likely outcomes of the courses of action open to us. The traditional name for this virtue, 'prudence', can be misleading nowadays, since it suggests caution, an anxiety to minimize risks. Sometimes, however, a bold venture is called for. Virtue is strength, not weakness.

We must exercise good sense with regard to the smaller and larger communities within which we live. In family life we need to communicate with each other and plan our life together wisely, so that the family is built up in peace, the parents are not overburdened, the children are neither oppressed nor undisciplined but are helped to mature, and the family's resources are deployed both carefully and generously. In social life, if we are voters we must think in terms of the well-being of the whole society rather than private benefit. If we exercise the demanding role of public power we must be aware of the aspirations and needs of those we serve; we must provide inspiring leadership so as to make public opinion more just; and while recognizing the limitations we face we must make policies that will promote the common good and international harmony.

Good sense allows us to deploy our other good qualities properly. For example, a man might by nature or upbringing have no inclination to eat or drink too much. This would normally help him keep to a sensible diet. But if his friends organized a surprise birthday dinner for him, it would not be sensible for him to eat a small portion and drink half a glass of wine. Good sense would help him see what the situation calls for: he must show his appreciation of his friends' kindness by entering into the spirit of the party.

A most important exercise of good moral sense is to form our *conscience*. Conscience is not a 'gut-reaction', nor is it the internalized parent-figure or super-ego of some modern psychology. Such a feature of our psyche may help us, or it may hinder moral thinking. Conscience is an *act of reason* in which we think seriously about what we ought to do (or, as we shall see in the next chapter, about what we have done). In forming our conscience we must consider the Scriptures, the teaching of the Church, good advice, and so on, and make a careful decision that takes account of the relevant laws and of the special features of our situation. Then we must have the courage to follow our conscience.

We have *justice* if we are determined to give to each one what is due. The context for justice is society itself, in which the common good is to be promoted and each person cherished. Because treating people in certain ways promotes the good of all, we can say that people have *rights* to those forms of treatment. To deny people their rights is an evil: it goes against the good of all, not just the good of those who are ill-treated, for failure to respect our fellow human beings demeans all of us. By justice, we respect the rights of others, and defend the rights of those who are weak or liable to be wronged.

A just society does not have to be one of complete equality, indeed it cannot. Certain people will have authority over other people, as a result of their age or talents, or through being properly deputed to govern. Different jobs are valued differently, and attract different remuneration, and in some cases at least this is fair. But gross inequalities, in which some members of society exploit others, are unjust and strike against the very notion of human community. Then justice demands that society be changed.

Justice requires us to respect the lives of other human beings, and their bodily and psychological integrity. We must preserve their good name and allow them to exercise appropriate responsibility. We must thank those who do good to us, fulfil our promises, and speak the truth. We are to pay our taxes and our debts. We have to obey those who are in authority over us – unless, of course, they command us to do what is wrong.

Respect for people's property is part of justice. The resources of the earth and of human skill are given us by God for the common good, but human well-being is best promoted if each person or family can be responsible for a certain portion of land or wealth. It also benefits society as a whole if goods and skills have an agreed price, so that a rich person pays the same as a poor one for a loaf of bread or the work of a technician. However, the right to property must yield to the greater value of human life itself; we are obliged to give to those in desperate need, and if no one will give they are allowed to take what they need for survival.

The State promotes justice by establishing courts of law in which wrongs can be righted and crime can be punished. The State is not obliged to try to eliminate every form of wrong-doing, only those that most strike at the common good and can be restrained without imposing something like a 'police State'. The courts must take care not to convict the innocent, and because they are to protect the good of all they should only use the minimum force necessary to deter crime. The same rule applies if the State needs to declare war in order to defend itself or right some grave injustice: there must be a good chance of success without inordinate suffering, only reasonable force may be used against enemy soldiers, and non-combatants must not be attacked.

Finally, we should act towards God in ways analogous to our acts of justice towards our fellow human beings. We must worship and thank Him, we must pray to Him in recognition of His power and will to care for us, we must fulfil our promises to Him, and we must respect those persons, places and objects which are seen as representing Him.

Courage is needed in demanding situations, where our emotional reactions might make it difficult for us to behave fittingly. We can react with unreasonable anger when we should be patient and oppose some wrong with gentle firmness. We can run away from evils we ought to oppose. We can even betray God or another human being out of fear. Courage enables us to react well when faced with challenges, or at least it enables us to take control of our emotions. It helps us preserve a balance between foolhardiness and cowardice. Its most striking act is martyrdom, in which someone faces death rather than deny God.

Self-control deals with the emotions that arise much of the time, just as courage deals with those that arise in challenging situations. We are not called to be unemotional, but our emotions can be unhelpful if they are not well-balanced, whereas they should enhance our lives. It is clearest with self-control that virtue consists in a balance, since we can go wrong by excess or defect. We can be greedy, or we can be fastidious. We can be lustful, or frigid.

In areas of food and drink, self-control helps us to enjoy what promotes our health and social intercourse. In the area of sex, it promotes chastity. By chastity, married couples enjoy sexual intercourse in a way that respects each other and the nature of marriage, and remain faithful to each other. By chastity, all people relate to those to whom they are not married with a warmth that is not flirtatious.

Self-control also requires us to behave with gentleness and compassion towards our fellow human beings and towards all creatures that might suffer. It promotes humility, in which, without false modesty, we are able to recognize the good qualities of others and give them space in which to exercise those qualities.

One of the ways in which good moral sense is exercised is in the formulation of *law*. By reflecting on what is good for us as human beings, we can arrive at conclusions of the *natural law*. Human authorities must go on from this to make rules for their own societies. For example, the natural law commands us to preserve human life. It follows that, when cars are invented, we must drive safely. In order to balance the need to preserve life and the need to travel, *human law* sets a 30 miles per hour speed limit in built-up areas. This is not a limit rigidly determined by natural law, for in other countries a 50 kilometres per hour limit is imposed, not a 48.5 kilometre per hour limit. But in imposing such a limit, human law is applying natural law to particular circumstances.

Note that law commands actions in certain kinds of situation. It cannot take account of every eventuality. An ambulance rushing someone to hospital may, if it is safe, drive on the wrong side of the road. The purpose of the law – to preserve life

– is fulfilled by the breaking of the law. The virtue that helps us
see when to set aside the letter of the law in order to fulfil its
purpose is called *equity*.

This helps us see that there is more to morality than obeying
the law. Morality is to do with *becoming good*. Law is a help in
that project, but we have to build up the virtues that help us to
do what is right even in situations where there is no law to
guide. We have to know when and how to do what the law
commands: even though God commands us to give alms, we
have to think how much to give, and to whom, and whether we
should put off giving right now because we only have enough to
pay someone his wages, and so on. Law commands certain of
the actions by which virtues are built up; it is the virtues that
make our character good.

God Himself has given laws. The Old Testament contains a
Law given to the Jewish people, and this includes elements of
the natural law that are still applicable today. The New
Testament, and in particular the moral teaching of Jesus in the
gospels, has been called 'the New Law'. But there is a tradition,
going back to St Paul, that Jesus has set us free from law. Of
course, the detailed rules that were meant to govern Jewish life
until the Saviour came no longer apply. But the freedom from
law the Spirit gives seems to mean more than that. On the other
hand, St Paul had to correct those who thought that our
Christian freedom means that we can do as we like. He demands
transformed, purified behaviour in Christ. If we realize that a
written or spoken law is given to a whole community, we can see
what is meant by freedom from law. A whole community
includes good, bad and mediocre people. The bad need to be
restrained from crime and encouraged to turn and be good.
They experience law as a form of constraint. But the good do
not. They do what the law requires and more besides, because
they are already attuned to what is right and fulfilling. Now the
Holy Spirit truly makes us good, with a divine goodness. He
attunes us to His own guidance. So, St Thomas says, what is
chiefly shown us in the gospels is not a new set of rules to
constrain us from outside, but the gift of the Holy Spirit who
moves us sweetly from within. Jesus does speak commands to
us, and we must take them seriously. But he also offers us the
Spirit of freedom, who can make us children of His Father, so

that by a kind of instinct we can reject what would lead us from God, and joyfully do what leads us to Him.

NOTES

1 Many 'tales of the supernatural' are not to do with the supernatural at all. They are to do with odd powers some human beings are said to have by nature, or with powers real or mythical non-human beings have by nature.
2 The two classes are not mutually exclusive. God can work through the psychological forces He has created. He can also allow Satan to do so!

CHAPTER 5

OUR NEED FOR LIBERATION AND FORGIVENESS

W E have seen that the chief purpose of God's grace is to lift us up to His own level, so that we can live as His friends and children and thus inherit a share in His glory. So great is this work, and so total is our dependence on God's grace, that St Thomas claims that our need for grace would have been just as great if there had been no sin. We do not need to emphasize 'the wickedness of us miserable sinners' in order to show up our need for God's mercy. But in the world as it is, many people experience oppression. Some suffer from hunger, or from natural disasters, or from sickness; some from ignorance or poverty. People are oppressed politically, or persecuted for their beliefs. We can be bereaved, we may have to cope with failure; even if all seems to be well on the surface, we may have feelings of guilt, justified or unjustified. For all this, and more, God's healing mercy is needed. His grace must come not merely to raise us but also to set us free and bring about the forgiveness of sins. It was necessary to speak about the *integrating* role of charity in the previous chapter because, in various ways, we are not whole and need to be made whole.

THE NATURE OF EVIL

Faith in God the Father Almighty can be put to the test by the experience of evil and suffering . . . But in the most *mysterious* way God the Father has revealed his almighty power in the voluntary humiliation and Resurrection of his Son, by which he conquered evil . . . With infinite wisdom and goodness God freely willed to create a world 'in a state of journeying' towards its ultimate perfection . . . This process of becoming involves . . . both constructive and destructive forces of nature . . .

Angels and men, as intelligent and free creatures, have to
journey toward their ultimate destinies by their free choice and
preferential love. They can therefore go astray . . . God is in no
way, directly or indirectly, the cause of moral evil. He permits
it, however . . . [He] knows how to derive good from it.

(Catechism 272, 310–311)

The evil in the world has provoked various explanations. The
Manichees mentioned in the Introduction, and similar groups,
have suggested that there are two sources of things – more or
less a good God responsible for what is spiritual and good, and
an evil anti-God responsible for what is gross and bad. In the
world into which the Church spread in her early centuries some
people thought that an impersonal 'fate' was in control of what
happened; some modern atheists would attribute the evolution
of the world and of society to physical laws, perhaps with a place
for chance or for human freedom, but no place for Providence.
Christian faith is placed in one only God, who has made, who
sustains and who guides all things without exception. If God is
good, and all-powerful, and is love itself, why is there so much
evil?

Some evil is *evil suffered*. This includes disease and death,
natural disasters, and the pain suffered from hunger, physical
attacks and emotional or psychological abuse. Now all this is
part of the working of the natural world, and an account can be
given of its place in the world. (I do not mean that it is natural
that people should attack or abuse other people. But it is natural
that we should feel pain when we are ill-treated.) These evils are
explicable if unpleasant. God could have made a quite different
kind of world, running according to quite different physical
laws – or even without laws, in which case everything would
happen by God's arbitrary decree and creatures would have no
powers to cause things to happen. In fact He has made the kind
of world that we are in, with its own particular beauty. It is so
finely tuned, as it were, that the age of the universe and its rate
of expansion allowed the formation of this planet and the
evolution of life upon it. The delicate balance of an environment in which life can survive implies a weather system in
which storms and floods, and periods of drought, occur as the
precise pattern shifts. The intricacy of living things implies
vulnerability: rather as a screwdriver is more robust than a

photocopier, because it is simpler and more basic, so a stone is less liable to be damaged than a spider, and spiders are less liable to be wiped out by climatic changes than large mammals. The balance of life on earth requires some living things to feed off others. The sensitivity of animals, which gives them a limited ability to learn, involves the possibility of pain as well as of pleasure. So when a cat reaches the end of its natural life, or a lamb is eaten by a lion, this is unpleasant, bad, for the cat and the lamb, but such events have their proper place in an 'ecosystem' that is good and beautiful. From the properties of fundamental particles to animal behaviour, everything fits together well.

We are part of the ecosystem. In one sense, therefore, our liability to pain, sickness, disaster and death is only to be expected. But we are uniquely sensitive, since in our form of life sensation and intellect, emotion and will, are combined. Our relationships with each other are more intense and important to our well-being than in the case of other animals. Therefore we experience physical pain more keenly in ourselves, and feel for others who experience it; and we are open to more subtle kinds of pain when others wound us with words, or relationships go wrong. We experience others' deaths as bereavement; and because there is an immortal element in us we experience their and our deaths as if an enemy were robbing us. So an explanation of suffering in terms of balance of the ecosystem and the valuable complexity of human life does not dispel the bewilderment felt when we encounter suffering.

The forms of suffering mentioned above call for things like heroism, compassion, support, relief and healing. They provide a context for some of the nobler elements of human life and society. To some extent this consideration can balance the keenness with which humans suffer. Perhaps *the* 'answer' to the problem of suffering is the suffering of Jesus Christ, in which, as we shall see, *God* shares our suffering. Maybe we should say: we share God's suffering. In the experience that converted him, St Paul (then called Saul) heard Jesus say 'Saul, Saul, why do you persecute me?' (Acts 9:4). Jesus was suffering in those Christians Saul was persecuting. Later, St Paul would write 'in my flesh I complete what is lacking in Christ's afflictions for the sake of His body, that is, the Church' (Colossians 1:24). We are called to enter in some way into Jesus' sufferings. I do not mean that we should look for suffering; it is Jesus' love we should try to imitate. But insofar as we do suffer we can see ourselves as experiencing 'the birth-pangs of the new creation' (cf. Romans 8:18–25) and as called to share Christ's journey through suffering to new life. God allows our pilgrimage towards Him to include sorrow as well as joy, and in some mysterious way this is for our greater good.

Some evil is *evil committed*. We can fail to care for the suffering, to relieve disasters, to heal the sick. We can actually inflict suffering on others, whether physical or psychological. We can damage ourselves. In fact, evil committed, *sin*, does not always harm others, but it always damages the one who commits it. It is always, at root, the pursuit of some lesser or illusory satisfaction which we prefer to a real and greater good. If I plan a way of spiting someone who has annoyed me, I pursue the pleasure of revenge in preference to the greater and more fulfilling good of forgiveness and peace. The one I spite may suffer in fury, or may react by forgiveness; but the distortion in my 'value-system' is a warping of my way of thinking, a cramping of my personality. I am damaged even if my victim is not.

Sin, therefore, is basically a deficiency in our thinking and loving. It is a failure to love and value the higher goods, so that pursuing lesser or imaginary goods leads us into distorted ways of behaving that do not fit with our humanity or our call to be God's children. It is foolish, irrational; but it is possible because of our freedom.

So we do not need to invoke some kind of substance or positive force of evil in order to explain evil; we need only point to the nature of the world and to the abuse of human freedom. God makes what is good, and does not directly cause evil. But He is indirectly responsible for evil suffered, in the sense that He makes an ecosystem in which carnivores eat other animals, and so He allows the lives of lambs – which He sustains while they live – to be cut short by lions. Without the sufferings that puzzle us, there could not be precisely this kind of world – and it is a world to thank God for. God is not at all responsible for evil committed, for sin, since it is not bound up with any good that God might want. It is a failure in love, which God merely permits to happen. The responsibility rests with us who fail.

Nevertheless, a puzzle remains, since God could prevent sin without destroying our freedom. In Heaven, sin is not possible, since the saints see clearly the goodness of God, and how He is our joy, so that their natural drive towards fulfilment means they freely and spontaneously love Him. In this life, God could direct our thinking from within (it would not be His way to force it from without) so that we never lost sight of His goodness and always served it. Thus even while we speak of God merely permitting sin, we can still ask why He permits it. A partial answer may emerge, in terms of the good that God can draw out of evil – not that evil contributes to the good, it merely serves as a context into which God can bring good. Nevertheless, we cannot fathom the mystery of evil until, in Heaven, we see into God's plan. Even then, we shall not see evil itself, since in itself it is a deficiency, not a creature of God. We shall see the corresponding goods, rather as the highlights of a painting stand out by contrast with the dark areas.

THE FALL

The account of the Fall in Genesis 3 uses figurative language, but affirms a primeval event, a deed that took place at the beginning of the history of man. Revelation gives us the certainty of faith that the whole of human history is marked by the original fault freely committed by our first parents . . . Adam had received original holiness and justice not for himself alone, but for all human nature. By yielding to the tempter, Adam and Eve committed a *personal* sin, but this sin affected *the human nature* that they would then transmit *in a fallen state*.

(*Catechism* 390, 404)

In Genesis 2 – 11 a story is told of God placing our first parents in a garden, where they succumbed to the temptation to 'be like God', and grasped at the knowledge they were not meant to have at the time. They experienced shame and were expelled from the garden, to endure a harder life, and eventually to die. Among their descendants, civilization grew up – and so did violence, pride and division. This story is more to be seen as an exploration of the human condition than as literal history, but the Church wants to preserve the idea that the human race is one family, descended from parents who were created as friends of God and who turned from His friendship, incurring for themselves and for their family the hardships we suffer from. In support of this we do not so much appeal to Genesis as to St Paul, who contrasts the way in which in Adam (our first father) all sin and die with the way in which in Christ we are brought back to God's grace and to life.

The idea that the whole human race is descended from a single first couple is not contrary to the theory of evolution. Science cannot yet show how many ancestors the race has, although attempts have been made to prove that we are all descended from one woman.[1] All the same, many modern theologians have tried to show that the essential elements of Catholic teaching can be preserved whether our first parents were two in number or many.

We do not suppose that the material universe changed its nature when Adam sinned. The garden in the biblical story could symbolize a special care God took for unfallen humanity which, coupled with the greater wisdom of unfallen humanity, would have preserved us from the physical sufferings to which we are now liable. We can say that if there had been no sin, human history would have been very different, and probably much shorter. Since, in His eternity, God foresaw and permitted (but did not decree or cause) the Fall, we might suggest that He chose to create a world in which a fallen race could be on pilgrimage to Him. The history God planned is a history of redemption, of rescue, centred on Jesus Christ the Redeemer. Some theologians say the Son of God would have come among us as a man even if there had been no sin; still, He could only come *as Redeemer* into a world in need of redemption. The supreme revelation of God's love, the death of Jesus on the cross, could only happen in a world of sin. So the *Exsultet*, the proclamation sung on Easter night, calls Adam's sin a 'happy fault', since it 'merited such and so great a Redeemer'.

In formulating the doctrine of *original sin*, the Fathers, Doctors and Councils of the Church spoke of the state of our first parents as one of *original justice*, a state of wholeness in which charity joined them to God, and by His gift all their faculties worked together in harmony. Their fall from grace was due to the sin of pride in which they sought to be independent of God and His guidance. This destroyed the charity which was the keystone of their state of wholeness, shattering the harmony they had enjoyed. Now Adam was the father of the whole race, and our nature has its source in him.[2] It is good that human beings form families and larger communities in which some people serve others by leading them; but this involves the danger of leaders' decisions damaging their communities. A ruler can be an inspiring figurehead, or can lead a nation into a disastrous war. So, in a sense, we were all in Adam, our head; but this meant that Adam's rejection of God's friendship, with its consequent loss of God's gifts, was also our loss. We should not suppose that God withdrew gifts from us to punish the whole race for one couple's sin, as if He were prepared to do something unjust in His anger. God allowed the whole race to lose certain gifts – which were never a right – so that we could receive greater gifts: the coming of His Son as Redeemer, and the ways in which we can share in His journey through suffering to glory.

The most important part of the doctrine of original sin is that we do not come into this world with the gifts we need, and so depend on God for restoration and healing. One can hold this without thinking that the gifts were lost in an historical act perpetrated by an historical Adam. But if there was an historical Fall, it is easier to say that God made all things well, and human rebellion has spoiled things.

THE HUMAN CONDITION

Although it is proper to each individual, original sin does not have the character of a personal fault in any of Adam's descendants. It is a deprivation of original holiness and justice, but human nature has not been totally corrupted: it is wounded in the natural powers proper to it, subject to ignorance, suffering and the dominion of death, and inclined to sin – an inclination to evil that is called 'concupiscence'. Baptism, imparting the life of Christ's grace, erases original sin and turns a man back towards God, but the consequences for nature, weakened and inclined to evil, persist in man and summon him to spiritual battle.

(*Catechism* 405)

What is due to us simply as human beings was not lost for us by the Fall. A new-born infant fulfils the definition of human being. But he has many years of development before he reaches adulthood and can take rational control of his life. Given the complexity of the child's emotional life, and the variety of influences on him from family and society, his development is a precarious thing. In fact, by itself human nature cannot achieve perfect 'moral balance', just as it cannot make us immune to disease and death. It needs extra gifts from God if it is to function perfectly even at the natural level of life in society, let alone reach its true goal in God. Without those gifts – lost, we say, in the Fall – human nature is sick, spoiled, wounded.

So we come into this world in a condition of need, lacking the justice – that is, the wholeness – that would perfect our nature. What is chiefly lacking is grace, a share in God's life, and therefore charity. Our wills do not, as it were, have 'God' written on them when we are born, and unless He draw them to Himself they are liable to focus on false goals when we are old enough to use them. So the forgiveness – that is, the undoing – of original sin chiefly involves remedying this defect. God bestows His grace, His life, and so, at the same time as the human being is made divine, the wounded begins to be made whole. We are drawn to God in love, our hearts are made upright.

Besides lacking charity, we also come into the world without the gift of complete harmony among all our faculties. Our drives are not always in harmony with reason of with our true needs. This 'emotional disorder' is called *concupiscence*. Without God's help we would be unable to govern our lives well all the time, we would be ruled by unruly drives. We are in need of being set free from the slavery of sin. God does this, first, by giving us charity, so that the basic direction of our lives is right. He brings some harmony into our psyche. He gives us enough strength and wisdom so that we can rule our drives. We become able to resist what St Paul calls 'the flesh', that is, the ways in which our desires militate against our true well-being. Concupiscence is not fully overcome in the course of our lives, which means that we face a struggle in which we can – with God's help – be victorious.

The struggle to grow in virtue involves effort and some pain, it requires *mortification*, that is, the 'putting to death' of wrong impulses. But while resisting wrong desires may seem like a cutting off, a dying to various satisfactions, it is actually a training that brings moral health and deeper fulfilment. Our goal is a harmony in which our instincts, emotions, reason and will all work together so that we flourish as human beings, though few achieve perfect harmony in this life.

Besides 'the flesh', we can speak of 'the world and the devil' as forces for evil, which because of our weakness we can only resist with God's help. 'The world' in this context stands for all the ways in which society itself can influence us for the worse. Society and culture are in themselves good, and make for human fulfilment. But in a fallen world they are marred and ambiguous. The biblical story of the Fall shows civilization and sin growing together. There can be 'sinful structures' in social life which pressurize people into colluding with injustice, and our concern for the esteem of others means we often adopt uncritically the values the media, or those we meet, encourage us to hold. God gives strength to His friends to resist false values and to make gestures of resistance to or repentance for the faults of society. He does not call many of them to opt out of society; most are to be 'leaven in the lump' – and the Bible does not show us a return to the Garden of Eden, but a pilgrimage to the spotless City of God.

'The devil', or Satan, is the leader of those angels who rebelled against God in pride, and seek to turn human beings against Him by manipulating the various psychological and sociological forces they have some power over (which do not include our intellect and free will). We need not work out which of our temptations to evil come from the devil, which from society, and which from our own psyche; we need only go forward in the strength of the love God gives us, trusting in His care and help, and making use of prudent means to correct false inclinations.

So our fallen condition means that the Son of God came as our Redeemer or liberator, and that His victory over evil has to be shared with each one of us. On our way to sharing His victory over death, we share His victory over sin, and this often involves some personal effort which gives us a more personal share in His triumph.

PERSONAL SIN AND LAW-BREAKING

Freedom makes man *responsible* for his acts to the extent that they are voluntary . . . *Mortal sin* destroys charity in the heart of man by a grave violation of God's law; it turns man away from God, who is his ultimate end and his beatitude, by preferring an

> inferior good to him . . . These are acts which, in and of
> themselves, independently of circumstances and intentions, are
> always gravely illicit by reason of their object; such as blas-
> phemy and perjury, murder and adultery. One may not do evil
> so that good may result from it . . . Venial sin does not set us in
> direct opposition to the will and friendship of God; it does not
> break the covenant with God.
>
> (*Catechism* 1734, 1855, 1756, 1863)

Once we reach the age of moral responsibility we can choose
good or evil. All of us necessarily desire fulfilment, well-being,
happiness; but we may disagree with each other, or change our
own minds, about where true happiness lies or what leads to it.
To commit sin is to lay some plan, or speak some words, or
perform some action, or refrain from acting, in a way that goes
against human flourishing, and reveals inverted or distorted
values.

We are not always responsible for our actions. We may,
through no fault of our own, be ignorant of some factor that
would make us behave differently if we knew it. We may be
unable to think straight because of fear, or extreme tiredness, or
the influence of some drug we have been given without our
consent. Psychological factors, such as addiction or some
ingrained habit we are trying to break, may diminish or remove
responsibility.

Those factors apart, our significant actions represent decisions that express our priorities. Sometimes we think before
acting, carefully choosing what course to take. In this process,
we may confirm, or change, our priorities. Sometimes our
actions flow spontaneously from our virtues or our vices, from
the character we have built up over time. Even if we act
carelessly, without thinking, a choice is still made – the choice
of the immediate satisfaction promised by the action in
preference to the effort of stopping to think.

We have seen that some actions of Christians explicitly speak
of a love for God. Others, such as fulfilling the duties of family
life, or of work, pursuing learning or other interests, and
relaxing with friends, are good things that enhance human life,
and are done by people with no special love for God, as well as
by those in whom charity is at work enhancing all these pursuits
of the good.

Likewise, certain actions are an explicit rejection of God. Those that imply a serious choice for the bad at the human level are also incompatible with a flourishing Christian life. God may be explicitly rejected by such things as faithlessness – resistance to the truth He has revealed – or a refusal to worship Him, or the worship of Satan. Sins such as murder, rape, robbery and slander strike against human well-being. In committing such sins, one prefers vengeance, pleasure, wealth or the like to others' and one's own well-being, which is promoted by peace, respect and community. A rejection of God is implicit in such sins, since they are not compatible with friendship with God. For we have seen that friendship with God means sharing His love for oneself and others. A man who defrauds people of their savings in order to buy a bigger car for himself, values a car more highly than the human beings God has asked him to care for.

Sins that involve an implicit or explicit rejection of God can be called *mortal sins*. They destroy friendship with God and lead to the loss of a share in His life, in those who were His friends. They put a serious difficulty in the way of receiving a share in God's life in the case of those who do not possess it. The term 'mortal sin' brings out the awesome dimension of sin. The refusal to worship God, murder, rape, and so on, would be seriously wrong even if God had not invited us to share His life and be His children and friends. But since God has invited us to this immense joy, to reject His friendship is both supremely foolish and a rebellion against his goodness and love.

Sins vary in seriousness: to destroy innocent life is worse than to damage property, for example. We should from time to time *examine our conscience*, that is, think over what we have done,[3] so that we can reject our sins and determine to reinforce our virtues. We must carefully distinguish *conscience* from *feelings of guilt*. We can feel guilty because of some embarrassing mistake that was no sin; and we can feel content and delighted because we have managed to put someone down or get our revenge in some way, when in fact we are guilty of deliberate cruelty. Because of the way human psychology functions, sexual sins are liable to excite feelings of guilt out of proportion to the actual guilt involved. Though objectively serious, they are by no means the coldest or cruellest of sins (except when domination or betrayal are involved, as with rape and adultery), and are often subject to mitigating factors. (Sometimes, of course, people can dismiss a really serious sexual sin, such as adultery, as a 'peccadillo', and blind themselves to their guilt.) We should not let failures due to weakness depress us; at the same time we must take care to avoid self-deceit, and resist the temptation to justify our sins to ourselves.

Law, which helps us to do certain good things, also helps us avoid certain sins. In fact, it is easier to put forward prohibitions than commands, to say 'Thou shalt not' (as many of the Ten Commandments do), than to say 'Thou shalt'. That is because there is more to doing good than doing what we are told. But certain kinds of action can be ruled out, because they are never the kind of thing a human being or child of God should do. When teaching people to play football, you give them advice on what to do, but they have to practise the game and build up skills so that they can play the game well. There is more to playing football than following advice, and on odd occasions the coach's advice must be ignored. But there are also rules of football, that lay down a basic framework for the game and rule out fouls. To break those rules is not to play football badly, it is not to play football. The virtues we need for human life must be built up by practice, and those we need for our life as God's children must be given us by Him. They enable us to live well. We are helped by advice given us by God in the Scriptures and through the Church's tradition, by various authorities, by our family and friends. We have to follow that advice wisely, and employ equity now and then. There are also certain rules that lay down a basic framework for our life, and rule out 'fouls'. We are commanded to believe in God, we are forbidden to murder. To break such rules is not to do badly in the business of trying to be human and a friend of God, it is to step outside that project. So mortal sin is a breach of a serious command or (more often) of a serious prohibition, in which our behaviour contradicts humanity or a share in divinity.

Because actions that are incompatible with our moral project are to be ruled out, we must hold that the end does not justify the means. For example, because human beings must cherish human life, and because those who imitate God the Creator of life must cherish human life, it is never right for us to kill the innocent. It is not the kind of action that should proceed from us. We must think carefully about how to achieve our good purposes, but if it turns out that we can only achieve some good by killing the innocent, we must abandon our purpose (we cannot, after all expect to achieve every conceivable good). That is why abortion is always wrong, and even if we are fighting a just war we must not do what amounts to killing non-combatants or endangering the lives of future generations.[4] Of course, not all prohibitions are absolute. We have seen that 'Thou shalt not steal' does not apply to those in extreme need, since it defends a value – property – that only makes sense as part of the sharing of resources by a community.

It is sometimes said that sin can only be mortal if it is a course of life which we pursue with settled determination. But a once-off lapse can also be a turning from God. If we take the relationship between a husband and his wife as a model for that between us and God, then the betrayal in which the husband leaves his wife and lives with another woman would be a model for the settled course of life. We can get into a mind-set or pattern of life in which we set up barriers between ourselves and God, and resist the breaking in of grace, the restoration of our relationship with Him. Referring to those who refused to recognize God's power at work in His ministry, Jesus spoke of *blasphemy against the Holy Spirit*, which never has forgiveness (Mark 3:29). To resist the obvious truth, to despair of God's love, to be hardened in sin, are ways of resisting the Holy Spirit, and from the human point of view cannot be undone. To God, nothing is impossible; He can break into a hardened heart and work a miracle of conversion. But the betrayal in which a husband goes to bed with his secretary on the way home from work would be a model for many mortal sins. He does not mean to leave his wife, and soon after his lapse he may feel remorse. Yet he has been seriously unfaithful, and at the time of his lapse he put pleasure with his secretary above fidelity to his wife. Likewise in our relationship with God we may sometimes be seriously unfaithful and put some pleasure or wealth, power or revenge above obedience to God. Such sins are mortal, destructive of charity; but they need not destroy faith and hope, they need not put up barriers to the gift of repentance. Even murder, committed in anger, may be followed by remorse as a basis for the return to God in sorrow.

There may be imperfections in the relationship between a man and his wife, such as arguments over finance, or the husband being grumpy over breakfast when the wife wants to talk. These do not call into question their loyalty to each other, their determination to stay together. Such failings are a model for the failings in our relationship with God that are tradition-ally called *venial sins*. These are not sins in the way mortal sins are; they do not destroy charity or our share in God's life. But they weigh upon our relationship with God, and dampen the vigour of our life as His children. They are like the faults which make people play football badly, people who at least keep within the rules, and are playing the game. When a misdeed is serious enough to engage a decision in which we turn from God to some alternative good (or apparent good), the sin can be mortal; but if we do not know the seriousness of the misdeed, or do not make a serious decision (because of diminished respon-sibility) then the sin is venial. Many misdeeds are not serious enough to engage such a momentous choice. We can quite often choose the lesser good without prejudice to a love for God above all things. If on a Saturday afternoon I can study the Bible or go for a walk, or sleep, it may be clear which of those three will be the most beneficial (it may not always be the first of the three!), and yet I may choose another out of laziness or misplaced zeal. But unless I am neglecting a serious duty as a result of my choice, I am not guilty of rejecting God even if I am missing the chance to grow more holy.

We must hold that those who are friends of God can resist temptation to mortal sin. Charity brings with it enough strength for us not to be disloyal to God. But the moral weakness that is in us as a result of original sin means that it is impossible to resist all venial sins without a special gift from God, such as was given to the Virgin Mary. Our weakness may be turned to good effect: insofar as we fall into imperfections that weigh upon us we can learn our frailty and need of God's grace; insofar as we can, with the help of His grace, conquer some of our imperfections we can gain a personal share in His victory.

Society itself is marred with faults, such as the neglect of the old or the failure to help its poorer members or other, poorer societies. It is difficult not to be in some ways bound up with all this; it would be very hard to counter by one's own gestures every form of social evil. Normally our 'giving in to the world', like much of our subjection to the 'flesh and the devil', is venial; greater guilt would attach to positive co-operation in cruelty,

injustice and neglect, or to a failure to oppose some grave evil
when we have a duty to do so.

THE 'PUNISHMENT' AND FORGIVENESS OF SINS

> Grave sin deprives us of communion with God, and therefore
> makes us incapable of eternal life, the privation of which is
> called the 'eternal punishment' of sin. On the other hand every
> sin, even venial, entails an unhealthy attachment to creatures,
> which must be purified either here on earth, or after death in the
> state called Purgatory. This purification frees one from what is
> called the 'temporal punishment' of sin. These two punishments
> must not be conceived of as a kind of vengeance inflicted by God
> from without, but as following from the very nature of sin . . .
> The forgiveness of sin and restoration of communion with God
> entail the remission of the eternal punishment of sin, but
> temporal punishment of sin remains . . . the Christian must
> strive . . . by works of mercy and charity, as well as by prayer
> and the various practices of penance, to put off completely 'the
> old man' and to put on 'the new man' [Ephesians 4:24].
>
> *(Catechism* 1472–1473)

Human societies punish certain crimes, in order to deter people
from committing them, so that the innocent may be protected
and society flourish in peace. Since we only have human
language with which to speak about God, it need not surprise us
that the Bible, and Christian thought, refer to the punishment
of sins by God. Sometimes vengeance or retribution is attributed to God; sometimes the threat of punishment is used to
deter us from sin. The forgiveness of sins by God can then be
seen as God releasing us from the punishment due.

   It must be realized that, just as 'God's wrath' is a metaphor,
so 'the punishment of sins' should not be taken too literally.
God does not need to inflict pain on sinners in order to satisfy a
thirst for vengeance. The fear of punishment can be a motive in
avoiding sin, but it is best seen as a fear of what we are doing to
ourselves. God's purpose is that we should become His friends
and children, drawn to Him by love rather than impelled by
fear. So if, in His wisdom and love, God allows unpleasant
consequences to follow sin, the fear they provoke is meant to be
just the first stage of a journey back to Him. Those who suffer
most by way of sickness or misfortune are not being punished

by God for specially grave sins; He may be asking them to share Christ's innocent suffering. The moral blindness and insensitivity we can get into is a more obvious, and more frightening, consequence God may allow our sins to have.

Those who love God are on their way to life with Him. Those who are in a state of mortal sin are on their way to *hell*, to what can be called 'eternal punishment'. Hell is a possible fate because God may allow us to condemn ourselves to the eternal loss of Himself. We cannot deny the possibility of hell, because we cannot demand that God draw everyone securely to Himself; life with God is not a due, but a gift He delights to give. And we know that we can reject God; most if not all of us are aware of times when we have seriously broken His law. So we must say that God could leave someone in a state of rejection of Him, while we must firmly hope that in His love He will draw us to Himself securely. At death, our souls pass beyond the possibilities of change that are inherent in this world of time; so any one who dies rejecting God remains without the vision of God for ever, wrapped up in his false goals and burning with frustration. If we embroider that bleak picture with images of lakes of burning sulphur, it is only to remind ourselves how foolish it is to reject God, the only fully satisfying Joy, in favour of some limited or fancied good.

The *forgiveness* of mortal sin should not be seen as God letting us off eternal punishment because we have come back to Him, as if our repentance placated His wrath, even though such imagery has its place and value. We saw towards the end of Chapter 1 that God cannot change; we can turn from His love, and instead of seeing His service as our joy and fulfilment, we can resent Him and His law. In His love, God passes over many sins, and instead of allowing them to destroy us, He rescues us from the hell we are set to inflict on ourselves. He frees us from punishment and forgives our sins by reorientating us, so that we once again journey towards Him. Even though most mortal sins do not put up special barriers to God, and can be followed by remorse, repentance in the full sense of returning to God's love, rejecting our past sins and determining not to repeat them, is not achieved by human strength, but only by God's changeless, creative and healing love. For it is the restoration of our share in God's life, when we have abandoned that share; and only God can raise the dead. So the forgiveness of sins is called, in Latin, *remissio peccatorum*, the 'putting away' of sins. It is God overcoming the destructive forces we let in, which we ourselves do not have the power to drive out again.

Besides 'eternal punishment' we must also speak of 'temporal punishment', that is, of a pain, due to sin, of limited duration. At first sight, it seems odd that temporal punishment is due to mortal sins that have been forgiven, as well as to venial sins, but it is so. The point is that all sin damages us, both mortal and venial. It brings distortions into our thinking, our priorities, our reactions, and so on; it blunts our faculties and corrupts our nature. Repeated sins reinforce such distortions. Mortal sin is forgiven when God restores us to love, but some of the corrupting effects of the past sin may well remain. Temporal punishment is not, then, literally a debt God exacts; it is the effort required to undo the corrupting effects of sin. It is analogous to the effort required to get fit after one has damaged one's health by over-indulgence and laziness; like physiotherapy and similar treatment, unaccustomed exercise can be painful, and so can the 'moral exercise' needed to enliven our Christian pilgrimage that sin puts a drag on.

The undoing of sin may involve the patient enduring of some suffering, or be furthered by *mortification*, by withdrawing legitimate pleasures from ourselves – not because we seek pain but because we need to counteract wrong indulgence. A gesture in the opposite direction to our usual faults is a kind of acted out prayer for balance and wholeness. The most important act of mortification is the diligent performance of our work and other duties, and learning to react pleasantly and patiently to the trials that come our way. The work of purifying our affections and attitudes is completed after death in *Purgatory*, for those who need it, that is, in a process by which God's love finishes perfecting those who die as His friends so that they may see Him face to face. God, then, 'forgives temporal punishment' by inspiring the process by which we are made perfect as His children and set free from sinfulness.

Not just any innocent suffering, but also any pain involved in the purification of our sins can be seen as a sharing in Christ's sufferings. A hymn speaks of the souls in Purgatory undergoing 'the shadow of Thy cross sublime, the remnant of Thy woe'. Our journey from the death or disability of sin to richer life as

God's children is a sharing in Jesus' journey through suffering
and death to new life. Sin may be allowed a place in our
pilgrimage because it is the context for a sharing in Jesus'
struggle and victory, pain and glory.

LIBERATION

There is no true freedom except in the service of what is good
and just . . . God blesses those who come to the aid of the poor
and rebukes those who turn away from them . . .

                                        (*Catechism* 1733, 2443)

The story of the Israelites in the Old Testament tells of their
oppression by Egypt and then of their exile in Babylon. From
both of these, God promises and brings about their liberation.
Many of the psalms pray for liberation from enemies, whether
individual or national, as well as for liberation from sickness or
death. We also hear God promising to set free the poor who cry
to Him from their helplessness, and the prophets spoke for Him
when they denounced the oppression of the poor and threat-
ened the oppressors with God's punishment. The same themes
appear in the New Testament where, for example, Jesus utters
blessing on the poor and pronounces woe against the rich, and
St James calls upon the rich to weep. This tradition has
continued throughout the history of the Church. She has
encouraged and engaged in many forms of relief work for the
poor, and encouraged the rich not simply to be generous
towards the poor but to practise justice towards them.

In the last 100 years, beginning with Pope Leo XIII's
encyclical *Rerum Novarum*, the Catholic Church has developed
a body of social teaching in which the issues of modern social
life are addressed and, for example, the rights of workers
defended. It has also become clear to many thinkers – Christian
and non-Christian – that in some societies the wealth and
position of a few is dependent on the exploitation of the many.
A similar fault can be seen to mar the relationships between
nations. Hence the growth of Liberation Theology, which
draws on the scriptural stories of God's liberation to provide
hope for those who are now oppressed. They are not simply to

be fed a hope for a better life hereafter, but a hope that can animate a struggle to right injustices in this world. In that struggle they are to be inspired by the values of the Kingdom that is, of course, the key object of our hope.

We must recognize our duty to work for justice; to acquiesce in the oppression of other human beings is sinful. Even if we cannot act ourselves, we must support with our prayers and by the expression of our opinions those who can act for justice. Liberation Theology is right to use the Scriptures, and God's promise of care for the poor, to give to the poor a conviction of God's care, and to encourage the rich to practise justice. Of course, unjust means should not be used to right inequalities. While this rules out terrorism it does not always rule out revolution; but there are occasions when an injustice must be suffered because there is no just way of righting it. Jesus, who was put to death by the authorities, promised that His followers would share his persecution. Therefore it need not surprise us when those who work for justice in situations of oppression are singled out for ill-treatment. Victory over evil is a gift for which we must pray, and for which we must thank God whenever it is granted. But those who are most clearly conformed to Christ are the martyrs, who are said in the Church's worship to share His victory, because they shared His apparent defeat with their faith unshaken, on their way to sharing His Resurrection.

When we speak of the liberation won by Christ the Redeemer, we are referring only partially to the overcoming of injustice in this world, achieved by work and struggle God has inspired. The chief liberation won by Christ is liberation from sin. This liberation enables us to live as children of God. It is available for the rich as well as for the poor, for the rich can be enabled to use their wealth justly and charitably. Not all are called to abandon their wealth, but all are forbidden to be enslaved by it. Our liberation involves the purging away of our vices and the (sometimes painful) growth of virtues. But as a rule it involves some share in Christ's struggle. This may take the form of a struggle against external evil, whether injustice or ignorance or disease. Or it may take the form of a struggle against internal evil, whether sinfulness or psychological problems we have to cope with without giving in to despair. The 'freedom of the children of God' involves some obvious victory over the forces of evil, and some sharing in Christ's suffering with our faith, hope and love intact.

DEATH

In a sense bodily death is natural, but for faith it is in fact 'the wages of sin' [Romans 6:23]. For those who die in Christ's grace it is a participation in the death of the Lord, so that they can also share his Resurrection.

(Catechism 1006)

In one sense death is natural to us, given that animal life naturally has a limited span. But since we are more than animal, with a 'part' of us that is naturally immortal, death is also unnatural, an enemy to be overcome. It is therefore right to mourn the dead, from whose company we are cut off, but mourning must be placed in the context of our Christian hope for a resurrection world in which life and community are restored in an enhanced form.

Because of sin, we are subject to death, though, since it is hard to see in what way we would have been free from death if there had been no Fall, some theologians suggest that death-as-we-know-it is the result of the Fall, with its pain, sadness, fear and frequent indignity. Because of Jesus' death, our death can be put to good purpose. It remains the last enemy for Him to defeat, but meanwhile it is a means of identification with Him. Jesus died commending Himself into His Father's hands, and we can die in union with Jesus, giving ourselves to the Father. Of course, few people are able, as martyrs are, to give themselves into God's hands so explicitly. In many cases, the moment of death lends permanence to attitudes formed earlier.

For those who die as God's friends, their love for Him above all else means that, in effect, they say 'You are enough for me, and if I can rest in You, I gladly leave all else behind'. But not every friend of God can say that without reservation. Because of our sinfulness, we cling to things, and find it difficult to give them up even for God's sake. So Purgatory is 'learning to have died', allowing God to prise from our grasp the things we only reluctantly give up for His sake. We become able to rest wholeheartedly in Him; then we can receive back life and companionship in His Kingdom, beyond the risk of any false attachments. Self-denial practised during life, is a kind of rehearsal for this aspect of death. Therefore we begin the season of Lent, a special time of self-denial, in preparation for the annual celebration of Jesus' death and Resurrection, by receiving ashes, a symbol of mortality. We are asked, especially, to fast, pray and give alms. In fasting, we counter our greed for pleasure; in prayer, we counter our proud self-sufficiency; in almsgiving, we counter our greed for wealth and our dislike of being disturbed by those who need our help.

Death is also the antidote to pride, the root of sin. We cannot restore ourselves to life, so when we die we must leave to God the work of bringing us to wholeness and glory. We must see ourselves as clay in the potter's hand, we must accept that we are God's handiwork, not our own. So death not only puts an end to sinning; if it is accepted in the spirit of self-giving in which we are called to live and serve, it renders secure the freedom from sin God has been working in us.

NOTES

1 The analysis of mitochondrial DNA, which is inherited only through the female line, seemed to show that all human beings have one female ancestor. Now it turns out that the 'family tree' the first researchers produced was due to the order in which they fed their data into their computer.

2 It was easier to speak in this way when it was supposed that the male seed plays the active role in conception, and the mother ministers nourishment. Eve's role in the Fall, preparing the way for Adam's sin, was seen by the Fathers as undone in the Virgin Mary, who in faith and obedience received Christ, the one who was to undo Adam's disobedience.

3 'Conscience' can also mean, as we have seen, thinking carefully about what we should do in the future. Then we speak of 'following our conscience'.

4 It may not be wrong to risk killing a few civilians by targeting a bomb on an ammunition factory, but the blanket bombing of cities, and the dropping of the atomic bomb on Hiroshima, are examples of war crimes. Weapons that result in dangerous, long-lived fall-out should not be used even against military targets.

PART 3

JESUS CHRIST THE WAY

We have seen that we have to live now as children of God the Father if we are to share the life of the Holy Trinity eternally. The Holy Spirit must come to us with divinizing, healing grace, so that we can journey from sin to the love of God and through death to the life of glory. It has been mentioned that this journey is a sharing in the death and Resurrection of Jesus Christ, whose suffering makes sense of our sufferings. In this part of the book we consider Jesus Christ, who fulfils all our needs most beautifully. He is the divine Word, the eternal Son of God the Father, who took our human nature and was born of the Virgin Mary, so that we can share His sonship and in Him become the Father's children. He made available to us the Holy Spirit, by His death and Resurrection, which are the channel by which grace comes into this world. They constitute the Paschal Mystery, the unfathomable event which fulfilled the Jewish Pasch, and opened the route for our journey to the Kingdom. St Thomas Aquinas therefore says of Jesus, 'As man He is the way for us to journey to God' (*Summa*, I, 2, prol.).

CHAPTER 6

JESUS CHRIST IS TRUE GOD AND TRUE MAN

EMMANUEL,[1] GOD-WITH-US

. . . the Church calls 'Incarnation' the fact that the Son of God assumed a human nature in order to accomplish our salvation in it . . . The unique and altogether singular event of the Incarnation of the Son of God does not mean that Jesus Christ is part God and part man, nor does it imply that he is the result of a confused mixture of the divine and the human. He became truly man while remaining truly God. Jesus Christ is true God and true man . . . Everything that Christ is and does in this [human] nature derives from 'One of the Trinity'.[2]

(Catechism 461, 464, 470)

IN the gospels we meet a powerful, attractive and challenging person, Jesus of Nazareth, who claims our faith. By His words and His deeds, and by the imagery and expressions of the New Testament, we are told who Jesus is, and what He does for us. But so deep is the mystery of Jesus Christ, the Son of God come among us as Son of Mary, that it is not surprising that the Church came to formulate her teaching about Jesus in the course of many centuries of controversy.

The doctrine we are here concerned with is the doctrine of the *Incarnation*, the 'enfleshing', of the Son of God. The word 'incarnation' is drawn from the statement in St John's Gospel (1:14): 'The Word was made flesh'. The doctrine may be summed up by saying that the one Person Jesus Christ is truly the eternal, divine Son of God the Father, and truly human, having been conceived in time and born of the Virgin Mary. He is true God and true man, and one being. We considered controversies over the divinity of Jesus in Chapter 2, and how the truths that Jesus is God and that God is one do not

contradict each other. The controversies over the Incarnation
were to do with the difficulty of accepting that Jesus really is
human and that He is one. The care taken by the Church to
settle these controversies was fuelled by the conviction that our
salvation depends on the Son of God sharing our human life.

Like the doctrine of the Holy Trinity, the doctrine of the
Incarnation is a central Christian doctrine. Cardinal Newman's
hymn that begins 'Firmly I believe, and truly, God is three and
God is one', continues: 'And I next acknowledge duly manhood
taken by the Son'. One of the most important days in the
Church's year is Christmas Day, which we observe as Jesus'
birthday. The time around Christmas is the chief time for
contemplating the coming among us of the Son of God. In
Chapter 2 we examined some of the ways in which the person of
Jesus is presented in Scripture and in the Church's tradition; at
this point we need to look briefly at the way in which the Church
came to formulate her faith in the Incarnation of the divine
Word.

One error concerning Jesus was to see Him as a human being
who *became* the Son of God by being adopted by God the
Father; this would go with a denial of the Holy Trinity. But God
is eternally the Trinity, and from His conception Jesus is God
the Son come among us as man. He is by nature the Son of God;
we are the ones to whom adoption is offered – and this adoption
as children of God the Father is a sharing in the sonship of Jesus
Christ, the Word.

Another error was to see Jesus as not truly human, and this
error has taken several forms. In the first letter of St John
people are already attacked for denying that Jesus 'came in the
flesh'. Perhaps because they saw matter as evil, these people had
(presumably) proposed that the flesh of Jesus was only a show,
not true human flesh like ours. Later, Arius, who denied that
Jesus is true God, is also reported to have denied His true
humanity. On the supposition that human beings are composed
of two distinct realities, body and soul, he seems to have held
that in Jesus the Word (the first creature of God) took the place
of the soul. In Jesus there was not a human psyche like ours, but
a super-human being operating human flesh.

After Arius's error about Jesus' godhead had been condemned, the idea that there was no human soul in Jesus was
perpetuated by Apollinarius. He claimed that in Jesus the place

of the human soul (or, in some of his statements, the place of the human mind) was taken by the divine Word. This error was refuted by St Gregory Nazianzen and his colleagues. He pointed out that 'what was not assumed, was not healed' (Letter 101). Human nature has fallen into sin, and the soul (where sin is chosen) is more diseased than the flesh. To heal our nature, the Son of God took our nature – and most of all had to take a human soul and mind so as to heal the seat of sin.

In the course of the fourth century, therefore, it was settled that Jesus Christ is true God and true man, with nothing lacking from His godhead, and nothing lacking from His manhood. The controversy of the fifth century was to do with how to express the unity of Christ. Nestorius, who became Archbishop of Constantinople, wanting to preserve a sense of God's transcendence, could not see how we can rightly say such things as 'God was born' or 'God suffered'. He was also concerned to preserve a role for the moral excellence of the man Jesus. These concerns led him to think of Jesus as, at root, two realities, a divine being and a human being, a divine Person and a human person. But, he claimed, they come together in one person, by means of the divine Person sharing His dignity with the man He assumed, and the human reality being lovingly attuned to the divine. Nestorius believed that in the gospels we meet one Person, one Christ, and he meant to preserve Jesus' uniqueness. But it was difficult to see how, on his account of Christ's unity, Jesus of Nazareth is Son of God in a different way from us, since in us, too, there is meant to be a co-operation between the human being and the God who dwells in us as in His temple. Because he was using the word 'person' (*prosōpon* in Greek) to refer to the outward presentation of some inner reality, Nestorius placed the unity of Christ at a less fundamental level than His twoness, and so jeopardized our belief that God's Word really did dwell among us.

Nestorius provoked a reaction by trying to stop people calling Mary *Theotokos* (literally 'God-bearer', but usually rendered in English as 'Mother of God'). His chief opponent was St Cyril of Alexandria. He used the same technical terms as Nestorius, but in different ways, so that it was difficult for them to understand each other. However, St Cyril clearly defended the (unfathomable) reality of the Incarnation. At root, Jesus is one single being. The Jesus shown us in the gospels is one Person, and in no way two persons. 'One must ascribe all the sayings in the Gospels to one Person; to the one incarnate Hypostasis [being] of the Word. For Jesus Christ [is] one, according to the Scriptures' (*Letter* 17, to Nestorius). Although he sometimes spoke of 'the one incarnate nature' of the Word, to bring out the uniqueness of the union between God and man in Christ, Cyril had no hesitation in recognizing the completeness of Jesus' divinity and the completeness of His humanity. He possesses the divine way of being, which the Father and the Spirit also possess; He lives eternally as God. He also took on a human way of being when he was conceived of the Virgin Mary; He was born, He died, He rose from the dead and reigns in glory as man. Cyril did not at all minimize the humanity of Jesus; he recognized that, as man, He was subject to hunger, thirst and pain, and he recognized that, as man, there were things that Jesus did not know. But he was concerned to emphasize that Jesus is *Emmanuel*, God-with-us. It was the divine Word who was born of Mary, though He was born as man. So Mary really is Mother of God. All that was done and said by Jesus was done and said – in a human way – by the divine Word. It was God who died on the Cross, though he died as man, not as God. St Cyril, therefore, preserved the astonishing truth that God really did come to dwell with His people, in the Person of the Word made flesh. His teachings were affirmed at the Council of Ephesus in AD 431.

When we say 'God the Son became man', we do not deny the changelessness of God. There is no change in the Son's divine way of being when He takes on a human way of being, rather as there is no change in God when my sins are forgiven. I may say 'God has forgiven my sins', as if He has changed His mind, but in fact I am the one who has changed. The Son began to be human, and grew as man, but that is because in His humanity He has been located in time. Nestorius' concern for the transcendence of God has not been neglected by his opponents.

After St Cyril's death, a monk of Constantinople, Eutyches, took his phrase, 'the one incarnate nature', out of context, and claimed that in Jesus human nature was 'absorbed' by the divine nature. This seemed to jeopardize the true humanity of Jesus, and against Eutyches Pope Leo the Great wrote a letter, normally called 'The Tome', in which he taught that the one

Son of God shares fully in the divine nature and fully in our
human nature.

> Majesty took on humility, Strength took on weakness, Eternity
> took on mortality. In order to loose the debt of our condition,
> the nature that cannot suffer was united to a nature that could.
> Thus, as the fitting remedy for us, one and the same Mediator
> between God and men, the man Jesus Christ, was able to die
> because of one [nature] and unable to die because of the other.
> So true God was born in the whole and perfect nature of true
> man, complete in what is His, complete in what is ours.
>
> (*The Tome of Leo*, chapter 3)

The Council of Chalcedon in AD 451 reaffirmed St Cyril's
teaching and affirmed St Leo's Tome. This Council established
the traditional terminology of the Incarnation: *Jesus Christ is one
Person, possessing two natures, human and divine.* We must not
misunderstand this formula. In the first place, the word
'person' does not refer to some 'psychological entity'. Nowadays, someone who wants to get to know me well might speak of
trying to get at 'the real person inside the shell'. This would be
to picture my 'person' as a kind of pilot in the ship, an interior
thinking and deciding being receiving information from my
senses and manipulating my mouth and limbs. If we transfer
that notion of 'person' to Jesus, we are liable to return to the
ideas of Apollinarius which the Church rejected in the fourth
century. The Church does not teach that in Jesus there is a
single thinking and deciding being of that kind, who has to
juggle information from 'divine senses' and human senses, and
has to handle both divine and human powers, like a pilot trying
to steer a plane and play with a toy car on his lap at the same
time. Jesus is indeed one being; in fact, to say that He is one
person is to say that He is one being. But this one being
possesses the divine mind and will which the Father and the
Spirit also possess, and He possesses a human mind and will
working in a human way, so that He has a truly human power to
think and decide.

If we interpret the word 'person' to mean 'a whole being', as
St Thomas does,[3] we can see how the statement that Jesus
Christ is one Person with two natures is not logically imposs-
ible. For there is more to my person than my human nature.
There are other features to me besides my being human: I have

dark hair, blue eyes, and so on. They are all part of my person. So it is not a contradiction in terms to say of Jesus 'There is more to Him than being God; there is also being human', or 'There is more to Jesus than being human; there is also being God'.

But we must not go on from this to another possible misunderstanding of the formula of Chalcedon. It is not meant to explain away the Incarnation, it is not giving us a mechanism we can grasp so that God's becoming man ceases to be a mystery. The union of God and humanity in Christ is unique, it does not fit into any of the phenomena that human science can investigate. We can state our faith in Jesus Christ, true God and true man; we can see how this faith is taught us in the Scriptures. We can see that our faith is not contrary to reason; but we must accept in an attitude of faith a mystery we cannot fathom.

We can propose analogies that pick up something of the Incarnation. One rather bizarre analogy put forward by St Thomas is to imagine someone born missing a foot, who is later miraculously cured. At the moment of his cure, something new comes into being, namely a new foot. But in another sense, there is no new being in the world. For the foot is part of the man who has been cured – it would not even be a real, live foot if it were not part of him. The number of whole beings has not increased. When we speak of the Incarnation, we must say that when Jesus is conceived, something new comes into being, namely His humanity. But in another sense, there is no new being; the number of persons has not increased, because the humanity of Jesus is the eternal Word's human way of being.

So the Son of God 'came down from heaven'. Without ceasing to be God, He took on a human way of being so as to enable us to share the divine way of being. 'The Son of God enters this lower world, coming down from His heavenly throne, and not leaving the Father's glory' (*The Tome of Leo*, chapter 4). All the teaching of Councils, and all the work of great theologians, briefly touched on here, were designed to keep before our minds the humanity of Jesus, His brotherhood with us, and the truth that in Jesus God has given Himself as fully as possible to our world. Godhead and humanity are joined in the unity of one Person. In His love, God has not been grudging, but has given the greatest gift He could, the gift of

Himself in the Person of the Word. Another of Newman's hymns contains the lines:

> O wisest love . . .
>   that a higher gift than grace
> should flesh and blood refine:
> God's presence, and His very self,
> and essence all divine.

THE VIRGIN BIRTH

The Holy Spirit . . . is sent to sanctify the womb of the Virgin Mary . . . causing her to conceive the eternal Son of the Father in a humanity drawn from her own . . . The Fathers [of the Church] see in the virginal conception the sign that it truly was the Son of God who came in a humanity like our own . . . Mary's virginity manifests God's absolute initiative in the Incarnation . . .

(*Catechism* 485, 496, 503)

In the Apostles' Creed we say of Jesus that 'He was conceived by the Holy Spirit and born of the Virgin Mary'. The first two chapters of St Matthew's and of St Luke's Gospels tell us of the events surrounding the birth of Jesus; and while we need not be disturbed by the claims of Scripture scholars that some of the details as written are more symbolic than historical, we must hold that Jesus was miraculously conceived of a virgin. It is the place of the Virgin Birth in the Church's professions of faith and in her prayers that shows that the Church believes Jesus was born of a virgin.

The doctrine of the Incarnation is different from the doctrine of the Virgin Birth. Logically, the Son of God could have become man in being conceived by normal sexual intercourse, and a saviour who was not God incarnate could have been born miraculously of a virgin. But it is appropriate that the Son of God should have been conceived of a virgin. For example, the fact that He had no true father on earth fits well with the fact that Jesus' father is none other than God the Father. Further, the fact that Jesus' conception is due to no human action brings home to us that He is a gift from God – indeed, God's self-giving – and a fresh start, the 'breaking-in' of God to a world that cannot save itself by its own action.

So to say that God is Jesus' Father is not to say that in Jesus' conception God took the role normally taken by the human father. That would make Jesus' conception like the conceptions of mythical heroes by pagan 'gods'. God is Jesus' Father because, in the life of the Holy Trinity, the Son was 'born of the Father before all ages', that is, He is from the Father in a way of which human begetting is a pale image. The same Son was conceived of Mary in a miraculous way that involved no male role, and was born of her by a new birth in time.

Although He has no human father, it is important that the Son of God took flesh from Mary His Mother. For this means that through Mary He is a member of our human family, He is our Brother. The gospels show us the divine Word sharing so fully the condition of those He came to save as to be born in poverty and to be taken into exile as a refugee from persecution.

We attribute the conception of Jesus to the Holy Spirit. In this, we follow what is said in the gospels, and recall the life-giving power of the Spirit spoken of in the Old Testament. The conception of Jesus by the Holy Spirit fits with the role of the Spirit in His ministry. For as man, Jesus received the Spirit, with whom He was filled from His conception, and in whose power He worked. But, as we shall see, He was to give the Spirit to those He came to save. This points us back to Their relationship in the Holy Trinity. For the Spirit, who is from the Father through the Son, comes to us from the Father through the goodness and the saving work of the Son made man.

JESUS IS THE MESSIAH

'Christ' comes from the Greek translation of the Hebrew *Messiah*, which means 'anointed' . . . in Israel, those consecrated to God for a mission that he gave were anointed in his name . . . Jesus fulfilled the messianic hope of Israel in his threefold office of priest, prophet and king.

(*Catechism* 436)

Jesus claimed that the Scriptures (i.e. the Old Testament) bear witness to Him (John 5:39). But the Jews of His time did not have a single, clear idea of what God was to do in fulfilment of His promises. Jewish writings that were not included in Scripture bear witness to a variety of hopes, and in particular to a hope for one or two *Messiahs*. The Hebrew word *Mashiah*, translated as *Christos* in the Greek Old Testament, means 'anointed'. Kings had been, and high priests still were, anointed with sacred oil, and the Old Testament speaks of prophets being anointed, though this was probably meta-phorical. There was widespread expectation that God would send a messiah of King David's line, some expectation for a messiah of the priestly line, and varied hopes for one of the old prophets to return, or for God to raise up a new prophet like Moses. More or less all these hopes were seen as fulfilled in Jesus during or after His ministry. The title 'Messiah' has been one of the most fruitful, and Jesus is often presented as Priest, Prophet and King. As Priest, He unites us with God by his self-sacrificing death on the cross. As Prophet, He reveals the Father's loving plan. As King, He defeats the forces of evil, sets His people free, and brings peace.

Many of Jesus' contemporaries had fairly worldly visions of what the Messiah would do, and thought in terms of political freedom for the Jewish race and defeat for their enemies, including the sinners in their midst. Matthew and Luke begin their accounts of Jesus' public ministry with a story of Jesus resisting temptation to be the kind of messiah many people wanted, John shows Jesus escaping from an attempt to take Him by force and make Him king, and Mark shows us Jesus trying to persuade His closest disciples that they would have to follow Him along the path of suffering rather than glory (Matthew 4:1–11; Luke 4:1–13; John 6:15; Mark 8:31–38). Jesus accepted the title 'Messiah' but was reluctant to allow its use, preferring to refer to Himself as the 'Son of Man', an obscure title or term found in the Old Testament and other Jewish writings. It probably had overtones of humility as well as of glory, and perhaps made it easier for Him to put across His own self-understanding without arousing unhelpful ideas in His hearers' minds. For Jesus was to fulfil the ancient prophecies in an unexpected way, in fact in a greater way than had been expected. By His suffering and death He defeated the forces of evil more radically that if He had imposed God's rule by force. He drew us to union with God by the power of love, and defeated the sinners not by destructive force but by turning them into God's friends.

THE HOLINESS OF JESUS

We must postulate habitual [i.e. sanctifying] grace in Christ . . .
First, because of the union of His soul to the Word of God. For
the nearer something receptive is to a cause influencing it, the
more it will receive of its influence . . . Second, because of the
nobility of His soul, which in its activities had to be most closely
joined to God by knowledge and love . . . Third, because of
Christ's relationship to the human race. For Christ, as man, is
'Mediator between God and men', as 1 Timothy says. And so it
was right for Him to have grace that even overflowed to
others . . .

(St Thomas Aquinas, *Summa*, III, 7, 1)

By its union to the divine Wisdom in the Person of the Word
incarnate, Christ enjoyed in his human knowledge the fullness
of understanding of the eternal plans he had come to reveal.

(*Catechism* 474)

Commenting on the ministry (and still more on the death) of
Jesus, St John says 'we beheld His glory . . . full of grace and of
truth'. This phrase, 'full of grace and of truth', can prompt us to
consider the knowledge and love present in the human mind
and will of Jesus – for we have seen that He shares our nature
fully, possessing human faculties that work in the same way as
in us.

We need sanctifying grace if we are, though human, to share
the divine life. Jesus too, as man, has to have sanctifying grace,
He has to be filled with the Holy Spirit. So in Jesus there is a gift
unique to Him, the union of God and man in a single Person.
But there is also a gift that is different in degree but not in kind
from the gift we enjoy. He is filled with the same kind of grace
which we are called to receive; and this works through the same
kind of divine love, charity, that is meant to move us.

In Jesus, the godhead is uniquely close to human nature,
since He is one being. Therefore His humanity is filled with
divine grace with a specially powerful intensity. His charity
towards His Father and towards us is incomparably strong. By
this means He can be the sole Mediator between God and mankind. Rather as a piece of iron heated in a fire can warm other
things, so the humanity of Jesus, aglow with charity because of
the divine nature within Him, can set others on fire with the

love of God. That is, when others receive grace, it is only through Jesus. St John says 'from His fullness we have all received'. The friends of God who lived before Jesus were given grace by reference to what He would do in whom they hoped; and the friends of God who live after Jesus' coming receive grace that flows to them through Him.

This truth, that we only receive grace through Jesus, is expressed by the parable of the vine and branches in John 14. We draw life only in and through Jesus; apart from Him, we can do nothing. It also lies behind the notion, found in the Fathers of the Church and in her prayer, of the 'wonderful exchange', in which the Son of God became human so that human beings could become children of God. By coming among us as man, but full of the divine life, the Word of God has made us able to share that divine life. He is the unique channel by which grace flows into this world.

The intense love for His Father and for us that burns in Jesus' human will inspires the devotion to His Sacred Heart. This devotion arose in the Middle Ages but was later strongly promoted by the Church to counter the movement called 'Jansenism', which suggested that Christ did not die for all. Against this, the Church emphasized the boundlessness and intensity of Jesus' love, symbolized by His Heart.

An awareness of the intensity of Jesus' love can help us overcome a common difficulty. Jesus is like us in all things but sin. His love for His Father was always so great that He obeyed His Father in all things with His human will. There was no room in Him for sin, and no room for any of the moral distortion that is found in us because of sin. But to say this can make Jesus seem distant from our experience, for our experience is of weakness and sin, repentance and forgiveness. In certain ways Jesus did share our weakness, for He shared our natural (and sinless) reluctance to suffer and die, and in prayer had to overcome it. But He did not sin, He did not need forgiveness or healing. So how could He sympathize with sinners? Note that our sympathy is limited by our sinfulness. For example, we may be indulgent towards people with certain faults, and over-critical of people with other faults, and fail to help both kinds of people as we should. Because of His sinlessness, and the great love which is at its heart, Jesus could relate to the people around Him precisely as they needed, and continues to meet us with

His patience and His challenges as we need. Jesus' sinlessness
means that He is more human than we are, not less, for sin
diminishes our humanity, both in the sense of distorting our
nature, and in the sense of weakening our love.

In Jesus God has come among us with healing grace, and also
with saving truth. He is the divine Word, the perfect image and
self-expression of the Father, come to reveal and carry out the
Father's plan for our salvation. His miracles, His death and His
Resurrection are revelation; so is His teaching. He is *the*
Teacher, and we are all disciples, even though He continues to
teach in and through the Church which is His body. So in Jesus'
human mind there had to be the truth He had to teach. We are
told in the gospels that Jesus learned, and that He did not know
the date of the end of the world; we also find Him claiming a
unique knowledge of His Father, and promising to share His
knowledge with others. The traditional way of accounting for
this is to say that in the depths of His human mind Jesus already
had the vision of the Father to which He is to lead us. Just as the
divine love overflowed from His godhead into His human will,
so the divine knowledge overflowed into His human mind. But
the vision of God is not a matter of concepts with which we
speak and think, it is a higher kind of knowledge. So from His
vision of the Father, in prayer and in reflection on the course of
His ministry and the ancient prophecies of it, Jesus had to draw
out those truths He had to teach us, and not those it was not
right for us to be told. So there were many facts He did not
know in the normal human way of knowing facts, though He
also knew much about those He came to teach and to save.

NOTES

1 In Matthew 1:23, the Gospel-writer applies to Jesus the prophecy
   of Isaiah 7:14, so giving Him the title *Emmanuel*, Hebrew for 'God
   [is] with us'.
2 A phrase used by the Second Council of Constantinople in AD 553.
3 He also points out that we reserve the word 'person' for beings with
   the power of reason. A cat is a whole being, but we do not call it a
   person, while we do call human beings, angels and each of the
   Trinity a person.

CHAPTER 7

JESUS' REDEEMING WORK

JESUS' LIFE, DEATH AND RESURRECTION AS THE CHANNEL OF GRACE

Grant that we may be sharers in the divinity of Him who graciously became a sharer in our humanity.

(Opening prayer of the Mass of Christmas Day)

When your children sinned and wandered far from your friendship, you reunited them with yourself through the blood of your Son and the power of the Holy Spirit.

(Eighth Preface for Sundays of Ordinary Time)[1]

The principal cause effecting our salvation is God. But because Christ's humanity is an 'instrument' of His divinity, it follows that all that Christ did and suffered work our salvation as instruments of divine power . . . Through [the fact that we were set free by Christ's Passion] we can know how much God loved us, and so be moved to love Him . . .

(St Thomas Aquinas, *Summa*, III, 48, 6 and 46, 3)

THE union of godhead and manhood in Jesus Christ itself has saving power. It ennobles human nature, radiating God's blessing on all who share the nature the divine Word took to Himself. The Fathers of the Church spoke of how, by taking upon Himself our nature, our birth, our infancy, our adulthood, the Son of God has brought restoration and healing to the whole of humanity.

When we think of this saving power of the Incarnation, we need to bear two things in mind. First, we cannot say that all human beings are automatically saved because the Son of God took on human nature. The grace that is in Jesus has to flow to

123

others, and this typically involves some action in which they are brought into some kind of contact with Jesus. It does not have to be their own action; when a baby is baptized Jesus reaches out to her through His minister, and plants the divine life in her. Even when an adult comes to faith and seeks Baptism, the initiative is not his: Jesus will have been reaching out to him through the Scriptures, or preaching, or some form of witness, and by His divine power at work in the convert's mind, creating his response to the message. We know also that people can resist grace.

Secondly, we must remember that the human race is fallen and sinful, there is evil to be overcome. Coming into such a world, the Word in whom the Father expresses His goodness was bound to provoke enmity. He could have undone sin merely by His presence, but in fact countered sin by the most generous means possible, by enduring our enmity and suffering on the cross. So the presence among us, and the whole life and ministry, of the divine Word has power to save, but that power is specially concentrated in His suffering, death and Resurrection.

The ministry of Jesus, in which He mingled with sinners, healed the sick and taught His disciples, was an expression, we might say, of God's homeliness. Besides the miracles in which the total healing of human nature was announced, certain actions of Jesus spoke eloquently of His saving work. For example, in Luke 19:1–10, a tax collector, Zacchaeus, is drawn to see Jesus, and Jesus invites Himself to stay with him. When people complain about Jesus being a sinner's guest, Zacchaeus promises to give generously to the poor and to anyone he has defrauded. In that and similar events we might see the power of God's love reaching out to sinners to create their loving repentance, a power which was to reach out most richly through the death of Jesus.

The gospels show Jesus' public ministry moving inexorably towards His execution by crucifixion, and devote a large portion of their text to the details of His *Passion*, that is, His suffering. He was executed by the Roman authorities at the instigation of the Jewish authorities, who were angered by His claims and afraid that if His movement grew stronger it would endanger the precarious peace between them and the Roman Empire. Jesus accepted His death as the culmination of His mission; it was His great act of self-giving. God gave Himself not just to be with us but to die at our hands.

Crucified and buried on Good Friday, Jesus rose from the dead on the third day, that is, Easter Sunday (using the inclusive reckoning of the Jews. The gospels record how His tomb was discovered empty, and, together with the Acts of the Apostles and 1 Corinthians, tell of how He was seen alive by His followers. The *Resurrection* of Jesus is much more than an act of resuscitation. When He raised the dead, they returned to the same kind of life as before, but when Jesus rose He went ahead of us into a new and greater life, beyond death and suffering – the risen life we hope to enjoy in God's Kingdom. Indeed, the Resurrection of Jesus is the prototype of ours. To emphasize the newness and glory of Jesus' risen life we are told of His *ascending* to the Father: apart from His appearances to the disciples, the Body of Jesus is no longer located within this universe.

The needs that the Passion, death and Resurrection of Jesus must fulfil are reconciliation and life. We must be drawn back to the Father from whom we have been alienated by original sin and by our own sins, and we must be filled with a share in His life. Forgiveness and life are the work of the Holy Spirit, who must come to join us to God in love. We have seen that Jesus' holiness and love, His being full of the Spirit, makes His humanity a channel through which the Spirit can come to us; now we must add that His saving work, His suffering, dying and rising, are themselves a channel of the grace-giving and healing Spirit. Through them, above all, the Holy Spirit is given to us.

This point is made in St John's Gospel. At the Last Supper, the night before He died, Jesus speaks of His 'going away', by which He refers to the whole event of His dying, rising and ascending. Only if He goes away can the Holy Spirit come to His disciples from Himself and the Father. Then, recording Jesus' death, John says (19:30) 'He gave up the ghost' – but the Greek could also be translated 'He handed over the Spirit'. In His dying, Jesus makes the Spirit available. Appearing to the disciples on Easter Sunday evening, Jesus breathes on them and says, 'Receive the Holy Spirit' (John 20:22). In the Acts of the Apostles Luke tells us how the disciples saw Jesus ascend into heaven forty days after His Resurrection; then on the Jewish feast of Pentecost, ten days later, they were filled with the Holy Spirit and began to speak the good news with power. This, too, shows us the new outpouring of the Spirit, greater than any previous giving of the Spirit, as the sequel to Jesus' death and Resurrection. Each year the Church celebrates Jesus' life-giving death and Resurrection at Easter, which is her greatest feast since it marks the completion of the saving work Christ came to perform. Eastertide continues for fifty days, and closes with Pentecost, the feast of the coming of the Spirit.

St John tells us (19:34) that after Jesus had died a soldier pierced His side with a lance, and blood and water came out. These have been seen as a symbol of the Holy Eucharist and of Baptism, the greatest of the sacraments by which the power of Jesus' death is brought home to us and the Church is built up. Recalling how, in the biblical story, Eve was formed from a rib taken from Adam's side while he slept (Genesis 2:21–22), the Fathers of the Church liked to think of the Church as the Bride of Christ formed from His side as He slept in death. The death of Christ, His self-giving for the sake of His bride, the Church, gives her life.

For many centuries Catholics have practised forms of devotion based on the sufferings and death of Jesus. In the Middle Ages, woodcuts were produced that showed Jesus surrounded by the instruments of His Passion. The devotion of the Stations of the Cross is still popular, in which events of the Passion are thought over one by one. In such ways, the psychological impact of the sufferings of Christ is brought out: the human suffering of Christ has a power to move us, to excite our compassion. But beneath this human power of Christ's sufferings lies a divine power to move us, to bring us to repentance, to create in us the divine love of charity.

Another popular image is the *pietà*, the image of pity, in which Mary is shown holding her dead Son. Her compassion is a model for ours; but since it was through her that the Son of God became a member of our human family, the image of pity also reminds us that it is our Brother who suffered and died. This, especially, should move us; but, again, because it is God who suffered and died in our human nature, there is a divine power at work in His suffering and death, able to impart the divine life to all His brothers and sisters who will receive it.

There have been no great controversies over the saving power of Jesus' death, as there have been over the Holy Trinity and the Incarnation. We do not need to examine doctrines hammered out in the course of argument. In one sense, we do not need to say much at all: if we say that the suffering, death and Resurrection of Jesus are the channel through which the Holy Spirit is given us, we have stated the basic truth of our salvation. It is an amazing truth that the Son of God should die for us, and we must hold it before our minds constantly. So in another sense we need to say a lot, we need to contemplate the saving work of Christ in our worship, our prayer, our art and poetry, and in our theology. In all these ways we need to build up a sense of how fitting it was that we should have been saved in that way, and we can ponder various images for ways in which Christ's work saved us.

THE RE-CREATIVE WORD

Christ's Resurrection – and the risen Christ himself – is the principle and source of *our future resurrection* . . . The risen Christ lives in the hearts of his faithful while they await that fulfilment.

(*Catechism* 655)

Two things come together when souls are made just: the putting aside of fault, and life made new by grace. The Passion of Christ and His Resurrection are each the cause of both aspects of justification, through the divine power that effects justification.[2] But as far as being an examplar is concerned, Christ's Passion and death are properly the cause of the putting-aside of fault, in which we die to sin; but His Resurrection is the cause of newness of life, achieved by grace or justice.

(St Thomas Aquinas, *Summa*, III, 56, 2)

We can become more aware of the transforming power that is in Jesus' Passion and Resurrection if we recall that He is the divine Word. It was through Him that the Father created the universe, when 'He spoke; and it came to be. He commanded; it sprang into being' (Psalm 33:9).[3] God's word has a power to fulfil itself: 'God said "Let there be light"; and there was light' (Genesis 1:3). The life, death and Resurrection of Jesus the Word made flesh are a kind of utterance of God containing the power to accomplish what is said. The holiness, obedience and love of Jesus are a declaration: 'Let my people become holy like my Son.' And Jesus' journey through death to new life is a declaration: 'Let my people pass through death to new life in company with my Son.' We have, in Jesus and His saving work, a *model* or *blueprint* that does not just reveal God's purpose but can draw us into conformity with itself.

In a fairly straightforward way, Jesus' dying is a model for ours. He gave Himself into His Father's hands, saying: 'Father, into Thy hands I commend my spirit' (Luke 23:46). We have seen that our death is to be a sharing in Jesus' death: He enables us to give ourselves into the Father's hands with Him, both during and at the end of our lives, and our conformity with Him is completed in Purgatory. Again in a fairly straightforward way, Jesus' Resurrection is the prototype, blueprint and source of our resurrection at the end of time. It is the cause of the resurrection of all human beings, but it is especially the model of the resurrection to bliss and glory of those who die as God's friends.

In a more subtle way, however, the death and Resurrection of Jesus are a model for aspects of our present pilgrimage, containing the power to inspire that pilgrimage. As we shall see, the pattern of Jesus' dying and rising is placed upon our lives by the sacraments, making more clear how all those who journey to the Father do so in company with His Son. Our turning from sin in repentance is a kind of death, for although it is a liberation from the slavery of sin it can be experienced as a giving up of some pleasure or apparent satisfaction. It is consolidated by works of mortification. This dying to sin is a sharing in the death of Christ which makes it possible. In fact all our sufferings can be united with the sufferings of Christ, and so rescued from the sense of futility they sometimes evoke.

Whenever we come to grace, whenever a share in God's life is given to us or restored after we have lost it, this 'new life of the soul' is a sharing in Jesus' rising to new life which is its model. Every victory over evil, and indeed every joy and success we receive as a gift of God, is lit up by the great triumph that is Jesus' Resurrection.

St John tells us that on Easter morning St Mary Magdalene saw Jesus in the garden outside His empty tomb, and at first

mistook Him for the gardener. Many representations of that
scene in Christian art show Jesus with a hoe or spade. The
artists noticed that St John means us to see that Mary was not
really mistaken. Jesus is 'the divine Gardener'. As the creative
Word He made our human nature at the origin of our race, in a
state of wholeness symbolized by the Garden of Eden. After our
nature had been spoiled by sin, the same Word came to make it
anew, and give it even greater dignity, which He did by His
rising to new life in the garden in which He had been buried.

THE WORLD JUDGED AND FORGIVEN

The power of the Cross reveals your judgement on this world
and the kingship of Christ crucified.

(First Preface of the Passion)[4]

The murder of Jesus reveals the sin of the world. His purpose
was misunderstood, the authorities feared Him, and so He was
done away with. This stands for all the times throughout
history when such things as misunderstanding, fear and self-
protection lead to cruelty. More deeply, it encapsulates all the
rejections of God, the times when His love invites and challenges us, and we thrust it away. Jesus is the invitation and the
challenge of God's love, made flesh, and was thrust away by
human beings. It is not the Jewish race that is responsible for
the killing of Jesus, but the whole human race, represented by
the Jewish and Roman authorities, the soldiers and the people,
who carried out His torment and murder. The death of Jesus
shows up the depth of human sin.

In that sense, therefore, the Cross of Christ is a judgement on
the world. In Christian art, scenes of the Last Judgement often
show the Cross held up in heaven as Christ comes to judge the
living and the dead. This symbolizes how the Judgement will be
the making clear of our own attitude towards the cross of
Christ: are we those who have put Jesus on the cross? Are we
those who have rejected God's love? Are we those who have
crucified Christ anew by cruelty to His brothers and sisters
around us? Or have we become those who have died with
Christ?

Jesus said He had not come to condemn but to rescue, to seek
out and save the lost (John 3:17, Luke 19:10). Much more than

a judgement on sin, the cross of Christ is a revelation of forgiveness. If we reject God, He does not reject us but invites us – draws us – back to His friendship. And the clearest possible sign of His forgiving love is the death of Jesus on the cross. There, God hangs, rejected by us, but still looking at us with love and not with anger, inviting us back into love, enduring our cruelty without retaliation. 'When I am lifted up . . . I will draw all to myself' (John 12:32). That revelation of God's forgiveness has the power to work our forgiveness, to overcome our sin and create love. But if we are drawn to love God, we are drawn to share the cross of Christ, to share His self-giving love and so in some way or other to share His pain.

You may hear it said that Jesus bore the punishment due to our sins, and this may suggest the rather grotesque image of God in His anger seeking someone to punish, not caring whether the guilty or the innocent suffer. We need give no place to such an image. We have seen that God is not literally angry; and it has just been pointed out that the one on the cross *is* God! The Crucified is not a man bearing the wrath of God; He is God-made-man bearing the wrath of men. His sufferings are not inflicted by God, but by us. So we may say that Jesus 'bore our sins'. But that means, first, that His rejection somehow encapsulates all the rejections of God. Secondly it means that He bore our sins *away*: He undid them by drawing us back to God in love. And thirdly, it means that He bore the weight of our sins, He undertook the arduous work needed to undo them.

Certainly, Jesus died to save us from punishment. Eternal punishment is being left in a state of alienation from God. Jesus was never in that state, but was always united in love with His Father. His death contained the power to draw us out of that state. Temporal punishment is all the effort required in the undoing of sinfulness. Jesus did not save us from the need to undergo some of that, though we do receive much healing from Him simply as a gift. But insofar as we still need to suffer in our growth towards wholeness, we can say that we are enabled to share in the pain of Christ, to share His journey through suffering to freedom. The cross of Christ is God's means of forgiving us, that is, of His overcoming sin. It is the channel through which God's reconciling and transforming power comes to us. It inspires us, enables us to put our sinfulness to death.

JESUS THE REDEEMER

The Scriptures had foretold this divine plan of salvation [achieved] through the putting to death of 'the righteous one, my Servant' [Isaiah 53:11] as a mystery of universal redemption, that is, as the ransom that would free men from the slavery of sin.

(*Catechism* 601)

In the social life of Jesus' time, one who had fallen into slavery by debt could be freed by some relative paying the required price. To redeem is to buy back. When the New Testament speaks of Jesus as *redeemer* and His death as a *ransom*,[5] does this mean that He purchased our freedom from God?

Jesus' suffering was an arduous work, undertaken out of love, and we can certainly say it deserved a reward from the Father. The reward was not just Jesus' risen glory, but our forgiveness for which He prayed. However, the idea of ransom, applied to the death of Jesus in the New Testament, does not itself involve the notion of a kind of transaction between Jesus and God.

For God Himself is called Redeemer in the Old Testament. In Old Testament law, property that had been alienated from the family that should possess it, as well as slaves, were to be set free by a kinsman paying the appropriate price. So the word for 'redeemer' could also mean 'kinsman'. When God is called His people's Redeemer in, for example, Isaiah 44:22–24, His closeness to His people, His care for them, is being emphasized. He is like a kinsman, just as He is husband, father and mother of His people. His power to set His people free, and His purpose of doing so, are also represented. But the notion of paying a price is left behind when the term 'redeemer' is transferred from human life to God. He has no one to whom He needs to pay a price, He sets His people free by His power, by which He can dispose the fortunes of nations (see for example Isaiah 52:3–6).

When Jesus is called Redeemer in the New Testament, a divine title and a divine work are attributed to Him. God's work of setting His people free is to be accomplished by Jesus. His closeness to His people, His care for them, is emphasized: He is not just like a kinsman, He literally is our Brother. He sets us free from Satan, sin and death, not by some kind of transaction, but by the divine power at work in His Passion.

So, properly understood, the title of Redeemer makes the dramatic claim that our Brother Jesus sets us free by dying for us. He is our Liberator. We are called to share His victory. We may do so by overcoming some injustice, or disease, famine or ignorance. But most of all we do so by living as people who have been set free from sin, that is, living by generosity rather than by greed, by kindness rather than by cruelty, and so on. And to live by those true values is to risk having to share Christ's suffering, which was His victory over evil.

THE HARROWING OF HELL

In his human soul united to his divine Person, the dead Christ went down to the realm of the dead. He opened heaven's gates for the just who had gone before him.

(Catechism 637)

In the art of the Eastern Churches, Jesus' Resurrection is never depicted, since justice cannot be done to that event which, in any case, was not witnessed by any of His disciples but accomplished in the still-sealed tomb. Jesus' victory over evil and death is represented by the icon of the 'harrowing of hell', which is also found, though with less power, in mediaeval Western art. In the East Jesus is shown, in majesty, often holding His cross as a staff of victory, breaking down the gates of hell and shattering its bars, trampling Satan underfoot and drawing out Adam, Eve and all the just people who had died hoping for Him to come as Redeemer.

This one picture holds together several realities, in the way art and poetry can. In 1 Peter 3:19 we are told that after His death Jesus went to preach to the spirits in prison, and the traditional interpretation of that mysterious passage is that He gave the rebellious angels a sense of their defeat and of our deliverance from their power.

From early on in the Church's history it was held that the friends of God who had died before Jesus' death could not enter the presence of God until Jesus had led them there. He must be first. It was supposed, then, that they were not in the hell of alienation from God, but in *Limbo*, a kind of waiting state, until Jesus could share with them the vision of God. It was held that Adam and Eve had repented and were among the friends of God in Limbo.

By showing Adam and Eve, and their family, in the hell of the demons, however, and showing Jesus setting them free from *that* hell, the icon represents the liberation won by Jesus for the whole human family. If we had been left in sin, and not brought back to God by Jesus' death and Resurrection, we would all have been in a permanent state of separation from God. Jesus has rescued us from the hell we were making for ourselves.

JESUS THE SACRIFICE

Christ's death is both the *Paschal sacrifice* that accomplishes the definitive redemption of men . . . and the *sacrifice of the New Covenant*, which restores man to communion with God by reconciling him to God . . . This sacrifice of Christ is unique, it completes and surpasses all other sacrifices.

(*Catechism* 613–614)

The final way of looking at the death of Jesus that we must examine is to see it as a *sacrifice*. In pagan practice it has often been implied that the gods' favour is to be bought by offering them something precious – even one's own child – and that such sacrifices can induce the gods to overlook one's sins. Do we suppose that we purchased God's favour by killing Jesus, or that He induced Himself to overlook our sins by having His Son killed? On the contrary, when we find the death of Jesus presented as a sacrifice in the New Testament, we must look for the meaning of this in the Old Testament, not in pagan practice.

In the Old Testament, God repudiates human sacrifice. He demands justice, and through the prophets He speaks against those who think that their lavish sacrifices can buy His favour when they repudiate His demands. He does not reject sacrifice as such; on the contrary, He commands or allows various rituals. Note that there is no single Hebrew word for 'sacrifice'. Each type of ritual has its own name, and speaks of a particular aspect of our relationship with God. Each is prophetic, looking forward to fulfilment by the death of Jesus which brings us into relationship with God. To call Jesus' death a sacrifice is not, therefore, to put forward a mechanism by which it works, so much as to point up certain aspects of what it accomplishes by the divine power at work in it.

Certain Old Testament sacrifices were 'peace offerings' or 'communion sacrifices'. These were a kind of shared meal, in which the blood and fat usually went on the altar, while the priests and worshippers ate the rest of the animal. These celebrations symbolized the community between the people and their God; indeed, such sacrifices were used on occasion to cement the covenant, the pledge of loyalty, between God and His people. Jesus declared that the new covenant was established by the shedding of His blood (Mark 14:24, Luke 22:20). We must see His death, then, as the greatest pledge of God's kindness towards us, containing the power to make us loyal to God, establishing communion between us and God.

Some sacrifices were offered as gestures of praise and thanksgiving. Some were wholly burned upon the altar, as a kind of gift to God. If they were a substitute for obedience, they were useless; if they were an expression of obedience, they were valuable – just as gifts we give to each other can be gestures of love or can mask deceit. Jesus offered Himself to God 'as a fragrant offering' (Ephesians 5:2), because His going to death was an act of obedience and love. Through it we receive the power to love and obey God, and to make our whole lives into a service of Him, which we can dedicate to Him in our worship.

Other sacrifices were designed to undo sins or the ritual uncleanness (not usually sinful) that debarred people from worshipping in the Temple. It is not said in the Old Testament how these worked; there is no evidence that the death of the animal was a substitute for the punishment of the sinner. The Jews would have had some sense of a mysterious power at work undoing sin, and we can say that the power to undo sin is channelled through the self-giving of Jesus, drawing us to God. On the Day of Atonement each year, the blood of a goat and a bull gave the High Priest access to the inner sanctuary. The Letter to the Hebrews sees this as prophetic of Jesus' passing through death into glory. He has gone before us into the true sanctuary, the presence of God, as our 'pioneer'; while His blood can achieve what the old rituals could not, a change of heart in us – the purifying of our conscience – so that we can serve God and hope to share Jesus' glory.

Finally, the story of the liberation of the Israelites from Egypt tells how the night of their deliverance began with the eating of a lamb (Exodus 12). The Jewish feast of Passover, involving the slaughter of a lamb in the Temple and its being eaten at home or in lodgings in Jerusalem, enabled the Jews as it were to relive this liberation year by year. Jesus is presented as the true Paschal Lamb; indeed, He died at Passover time. His cross and Resurrection are His and our journey through death to new life; they free us from slavery to sin and ultimately from death itself. On our pilgrimage to the life Jesus won for us, we are enabled to enter into, to 'relive' His Paschal Mystery by our celebration of the Holy Eucharist, which fulfils for us the role the Passover fulfilled for the Jews, and does more besides.

NOTES

1 From the Roman Missal, ICEL translation.
2 'Justification', being made just, is taken by St Thomas from the Latin version of St Paul's Letters, and is used by him for the change God works in us when grace comes so that we turn from sin to God and our sins are forgiven.
3 *The Psalms, A New Translation*, The Grail (Collins, London, 1963).
4 From the Roman Missal, ICEL translation.
5 See, for example, Mark 10:45; Luke 24:21; 1 Peter 1:18–19; Hebrews 9:12.

PART 4

BEING BUILT UP INTO CHRIST

It is through the saving work of Jesus Christ that we receive the Holy Spirit, who joins us to God the Father as His children, and sets us free from our sins. He draws us together as God's people, and makes us members of Christ, for it is Christ's sonship we share, Christ's holiness we are to imitate. But Jesus' saving work was carried out in Palestine 2,000 years ago. The people around Him could hear Him, even be touched by Him. In what ways can He reach out to us in our own place and time, to speak to us, touch us, bring the power of His death and Resurrection to bear on us? How can we be one with the disciples on whom He breathed, saying, 'Receive the Holy Spirit'?

Jesus has reached out to people of every place and time, often in hidden ways. To His own Jewish people He had reached out for over 1,000 years through the Law, prophecies and ritual that spoke of Him. More powerfully still, He has reached out for the last 2,000 years through the life and witness of His followers, He has spoken to people through the Scriptures we have preserved and made available, and, above all, He has touched people through the sacraments. In all these ways He has drawn people to His Father, He has given them His Spirit. In the last part of this book, we look at the sacraments and what they tell us about the life of the Church in which Jesus' words are cherished and in which the Spirit is at work making us Christ's members.

CHAPTER 8

THE HOLY EUCHARIST

THE RITE OF MASS, HEART OF THE LITURGY

In the Church's liturgy the divine blessing is fully revealed and communicated. The Father is acknowledged and adored as the source and the end of all the blessings of creation and salvation. In his Word who became incarnate, died, and rose for us, he fills us with his blessings. Through his Word, he pours into our hearts the Gift that contains all gifts, the Holy Spirit . . . The Eucharist is the sum and summary of our faith . . . The inexhaustible richness of this sacrament is expressed in the different names we give it . . .:

Eucharist, because it is an action of thanksgiving to God. The Greek words *eucharistein* [Luke 22:19; 1 Corinthians 11:24] and *eulogein* [Matthew 26:26; Mark 14:22] recall the Jewish blessings that proclaim – especially during a meal – God's works: creation, redemption and sanctification.

The *Lord's Supper,* because of its connection with the supper which the Lord took with his disciples on the eve of his Passion, and because it anticipates the *wedding feast of the Lamb* in the heavenly Jerusalem.

The *Breaking of Bread,* because Jesus used this rite, part of a Jewish meal, when . . . he blessed and distributed . . .

Eucharistic assembly . . . memorial . . . Holy Sacrifice . . . Holy and Divine Liturgy . . . Sacred Mysteries . . . the Most Blessed Sacrament . . . Holy Communion . . . bread from heaven, medicine of immortality, viaticum . . . Holy Mass . . .

(*Catechism* 1082, 1327–1332)

THE central Christian act of worship is the *Holy Eucharist.* In the Roman Catholic Church this is usually called the *Mass.*[1] In the Eastern Churches[2] it is called 'the liturgy' (i.e.

'service'), but in the West the term *liturgy* came to be used of the whole of the Church's official, public worship. The Second Vatican Council said: 'The Liturgy is the summit toward which the activity of the Church is directed; at the same time it is the fountain from which all her power flows.' The same Council called the Eucharist 'the fount and apex of the whole Christian life' (*Constitution on the Sacred Liturgy*, 10; *Dogmatic Constitution on the Church*, 11). The Eucharist is the heart of the liturgy, and the liturgy is the heart of the Church's *contemplation*. Contemplation is basically looking at God the Father as He shows Himself to us in His Word, it is to ponder in a spirit of faith the things Jesus said, did and suffered in order to show us God's love. These things are held before us in the liturgy, as each year the story of Jesus is unfolded, as we hear and sing the words of Scripture, and as the sacraments bring home to us the saving events of 2,000 years ago. We are inspired by the liturgy to go on pondering God's revelation by reading the Scriptures, by studying theology, and by prayerful meditation; we are charged to show to others, by word and deed, the love we have been shown. We come back to the liturgy, in company with those we have won for Christ, bringing our successes and our failures, our joys and sorrows, so that they may be given meaning in the light of Jesus' death and Resurrection. It should not surprise us if the Church's official worship does not always seem very 'contemporary', for while it is important to present the Gospel message attractively with the help of modern insights and concerns, it is more important to bring our insights and concerns to be judged in the light of God's revelation. If we are prepared to let it form our consciousness, the Liturgy cannot fail to be meaningful, for it presents us with the ultimate source of meaning, Christ's cross. Because it contains the creative Word, whose Paschal sacrifice heals creation and can make our life into a journey to God, the Mass makes sense of everything.

The word 'Eucharist' means 'thanksgiving', and this points us back to the origin of the rite. The night before His death, Jesus celebrated the *Last Supper* with His disciples. Following the Jewish custom, He took a cup of wine before the meal, gave thanks and shared it.[3] Then He took bread, gave thanks, broke it and gave it to the disciples, saying, 'This is my body which is given for you.' After the meal, he again followed the custom of giving thanks over a cup of wine, and of this cup He said, 'This cup is the new covenant in my blood.'[4] This Jewish ritual was already laden with symbolism. The shared bread brings before the company God's gift of creation. Because the vine was an image for the people whom God had 'planted', the shared wine was a symbol of God's gathering His people and giving them life and joy. The thanksgiving spoken over the cup naturally continued with a prayer for God to complete His work of gathering His people. Building on all this, Jesus gave further meaning to the bread and the cup. In the bread that becomes Jesus' body, God's gift of a new creation – centred on that crucified and risen body – is brought home to us. Jesus shed His blood on the cross to establish the New Covenant, that is, to show us God's loyalty to us and create our loyalty to God, and so He gathered into one the scattered children of God (John 11:52). This Covenant is shown us, and the reconciling work is continued, in the wine that becomes Christ's blood.

Despite changes of detail, despite local variations, and despite the fact that it can be celebrated with great pomp or very simply, the basic structure of the Mass was fixed very early, and has remained the same since. The first Christians celebrated the Eucharist in conjunction with a shared meal, but this soon dropped out, leaving the ritual thanksgiving over bread and wine that Jesus had commanded us to do in His memory, preceded by Scripture readings and combined with prayers such as the 'Our Father' Jesus taught. Thus the 'Liturgy of the Eucharist' is preceded by the 'Liturgy of the Word'. The shape of the Mass owes much to the Jewish synagogue worship familiar to the first Christians. But at its heart the priest who presides in Christ's role does what Christ did. He takes bread and wine, and recites over them a prayer of thanksgiving (a Eucharistic Prayer) which begins with the words Jesus would have used: 'Let us give thanks to the Lord our God.' In the course of this prayer the priest speaks a form of the words Jesus spoke: 'This is my body, which will be given up for you. This is the cup of my blood, the blood of the new and everlasting covenant. . . '[5] This is the *Consecration*, in which the bread and wine become the body and blood of Christ. The priest continues with the Breaking of the Bread and the giving of *Holy Communion*, as Jesus broke and gave.

Many details of the rite of mass bear witness to its 'roots' and its history. The Hebrew words *Amen* ('So be it'), *Alleluia* ('Praise the Lord') and *Hosanna* ('Grant salvation'), and some of the melodies of the Gregorian chant, which the Church holds in high esteem, are taken from Jewish worship. Some water is mixed with the wine that is brought to the altar, following the everyday practice of the first century; this mixing of wine and water came to be seen as a symbol of the union between godhead and humanity in Christ. The robes of the priest and other ministers evolved from everyday and ceremonial garments of the Roman Empire, while the Greek phrase *Kyrie, eleison* ('Lord, have mercy') reminds us of a time when Greek was the common language of the Mediterranean world. In the Western part of the Empire Latin came to be used in the liturgy. Since the 1960s the people's own language has been used for much or all of most Masses, but the Church still encourages the use of Latin, to evoke a sense of continuity with past ages and with the universal Church. The prayers composed in Latin, and the music composed or adapted for them, are a precious heritage.

The liturgy has incorporated features common to many religions, such as gestures, music, candles, incense and religious art; pagan places of worship have sometimes been made into Christian churches. The way in which the liturgy can be a home for human skills and instincts illustrates how grace builds on nature; it inspires us to use our skills in justice and charity, and, as necessary, purifies our instincts. A concern to make clear the difference between Christian and pagan worship balanced the Church's use of pre-Christian elements. She did not build temples of the pagan kind. They were houses for the gods; the worshippers gathered outside. But the Christian churches, like Jewish synagogues, were places for God's people to assemble. The creator of the whole universe cannot be tied down to a place – yet His people are His temple! He dwells in their hearts, and in the holiness of their lives they worship Him wherever they are, in the strength of the Spirit whose presence is renewed in the liturgy.

Catholics are asked to attend Mass on Sunday, the day of Jesus' Resurrection, and on a few other important days each year,[6] if they can. They are asked to receive Holy Communion at least once a year, and that near Easter, but are encouraged to receive much more frequently. Those two obligations are not to be seen as impositions: it should be our delight to celebrate Jesus' victory as the people He has set free, and to receive the gift of Himself.

THE SACRED SCRIPTURES

Sacred Scripture is of paramount importance in the celebration of the Liturgy.

(Vatican II, *Constitution on the Sacred Liturgy*, 24)

In Sacred Scripture, the Church constantly finds her nourishment and her strength, for she welcomes it not as a human word, 'but as what it really is, the word of God' . . . 'To compose the sacred books, God chose certain men who, all the while he employed them in this task, made full use of their own faculties and powers so that, though he acted in them and by them, it was as true authors that they were consigned to writing whatever he wanted written, and no more' . . . In order to discover *the sacred authors' intention*, the reader must take into account the conditions of their time and culture, the literary genres in use at that time, and the modes of feeling, speaking and narrating then current . . . But since Sacred Scripture is inspired . . . '[it] must be read and interpreted in the light of the same Spirit by whom it was written.'

(*Catechism* 104, 106, 110, 111,
quoting Vatican II,
Dogmatic Constitution on Divine Revelation,
11 and 12)

The Bible is read at Mass, and nothing else may be read in its place. The readings end: *Verbum Domini* ('the word of the Lord'). The Church's liturgy shows how much she values the Scriptures, and especially the gospels. But can we really call each passage of the Bible 'a word of the Lord'? In the time of the early Church, the heretic Marcion rejected the Old Testament. Later, St Augustine had to defend Scriptures whose 'barbarous' style had once put him off. At the time of the Reformation the Protestants rejected the authority of certain books and passages which the Jews had not allowed into the Hebrew Old Testament but which the Catholic Church declared to be inspired by God. More recently, the historicity of many events recorded in the Bible has been challenged, and this has been seen as devaluing it. At the same time much valuable research has been carried out on the process in which the Bible was composed, and an understanding of that process of composition, collection and editing can help us value the Bible and draw meaning from it.

When we come to consider how God has revealed Himself, we should begin by recalling that Jesus Christ is *the* Word of God. The Father's self-revelation took place in person rather than in a form of words. But Jesus is the centre and key of the whole history in which God's work of salvation is carried out; the Scriptures are meant to help us see the history of salvation moving to its climax in Christ, they tell us who He is, and they enable us to see our own lives as part of the on-going story of salvation. Since Jesus speaks in them, the Scriptures can be seen as the key to the history in which they have been composed and preserved.

To say that the Scriptures are inspired by God is to claim Him as their true Author. It is not to imply that the Holy Spirit dictated them word by word to 'secretaries' who were insulated from the on-going history of salvation. The Spirit guided that history in the intimate way only God can, so that as it unfolded, these writings were formed, fit for their role. Sometimes it was clear that God was revealing Himself; for example, miracles are recorded, and on occasion a prophet knew that he had a message from God. Often, human words were spoken, written and edited without the men and women involved clearly knowing that they were inspired. Looking back with the help of faith the Church could recognize God's words recorded under His guidance.

It has long been known that the Scriptures can be interpreted in many valid ways. The Jewish Rabbis used several approaches, and tried to preserve the variant readings that had crept into the text, since each might contain a helpful message. Christian scholars have recognized a 'literal meaning' in Scripture, the 'surface message' if you like – which might already be symbolic, since the Bible contains some stories which clearly, or on reflection, can be seen as meant symbolically. Much 'allegorical' interpretation has also been employed, particularly the *typology* whereby Old Testament events were seen as prophesying the life, death and Resurrection of Jesus. Moral lessons, and hopes for the future, have also been drawn out of Scripture.

An awareness of this richness of interpretation should warn us against fundamentalism, in which one sticks to a rigid, over-literal interpretation, and is afraid of subtlety and of scientific scholarship, as if that could be contrary to faith.

By showing us the process in which the Scriptures were composed, scholarly research can help us see what some biblical idea meant in its original concept. We can see new depths in the biblical images, put forward by people who drew on their background or reacted against it. Passages of Scripture can come alive when we see how they expressed or supported faith and hope when they were first spoken or written, when they were preserved, when they were re-used, and when they were placed in the context in which we find them. We can see how prophets sometimes uttered messages received in visions, and how they were often moved to speak by events or injustices they witnessed. We can observe poets and sages, story-tellers and historians seeking to understand life and death, success and disaster. We listen to worshippers bringing their needs before God, and to the words of consolation spoken in reply. We can understand why prophets and law-givers fought for the fidelity of their people to the true God and His demands, attacking the false gods and the false morality of those who worshipped them. We can recognize what battles St Paul was fighting, and put his letters in their proper context. The concern of the gospel-writers to help others come to faith in Jesus and to bring out the (often uncomfortable) meaning of His ministry for their fellow-Christians is made clearer. Scientific historical or literary methods can be applied to this human process, for, as we saw in Chapter 1, God is at work in all that happens, not in opposition to created causes, but as their transcendent guide.

Since it is a scientific discipline,[7] the findings of Scripture scholarship are hypotheses that need to be tested and are open to revision. In the physical sciences, certain theories were held for a long time because of the authority of figures like Newton, or through being much repeated, that in the end had to give way before evidence or argument. In Scripture scholarship there is a similar danger of relying too much on the authority of great scholars or on common opinions, and a greater danger of 'hidden agendas'. For in this area a prejudice against the miraculous may lead to misinterpretations: if it is supposed that a miracle recorded in Scripture could not have happened, the biblical authors who were concerned to tell us what took place may be seen as having composed a symbolic story. We should bring to the Bible the critical faculties God has given us – aided by His gift of faith.

Discussing some of the fanciful interpretations of Scripture sometimes put forward, St Augustine pointed out that the important thing is to build up faith, hope and charity. It is interpretations that destroy those virtues that we should beware of. So we must read the Scriptures within the community of faith and charity during whose earlier history they were composed, that is, within the Church, who preserves in her Creeds the main lines of the scriptural message.

PRAYER

Christian prayer is a covenant relationship between God and man in Christ. It is the action of God and of man, springing forth from both the Holy Spirit and ourselves, wholly directed to the Father, in union with the human will of the Son of God made man . . . When we share in God's saving love, we understand that *every need* can become the object of petition. Christ, who assumed all things in order to redeem all things, is glorified by what we ask the Father in his name . . . The Tradition of the Church proposes to the faithful certain rhythms of praying intended to nourish continual prayer. Some are daily, such as morning and evening prayer, grace before and after meals, the Liturgy of the Hours . . . [In] the Liturgy of the Hours, 'the divine office' . . . [the] 'public prayer of the Church', the faithful . . . exercise the royal priesthood of the baptized . . . 'the voice of the Bride herself addressed to her Bridegroom. It is the very prayer which Christ himself together with his Body addresses to the Father.'

(*Catechism* 2564, 2633, 2698, 1174; quoting
Vatican II, *Constitution on the Sacred Liturgy*, 84)

The Mass is the highest form of *prayer*, it reminds us to pray, and it sheds light on all our prayer. The word 'prayer' originally meant *petition*, but it can also be used to cover all the ways in which we *talk to God*. It is most important to talk to God, since talking to each other is a gesture of friendship and supports friendship. God of course talks to us: He answers our prayer, but more fundamentally, He speaks to us first, and we reply; in fact, our prayer is prompted by the Holy Spirit, and a sign of that is the way in which the Church often prays in the words of the Psalms the Spirit Himself inspired.

Justice demands that we praise God and thank Him; and the Mass is at heart *the* act of thanksgiving. As such it is the anticipation of the eternal praise and thanksgiving of heaven, and a sharing in the Son's worship of the Father. It reminds us to praise and thank God at all times, with our hearts and voices, and so to make our whole lives into a service of God.

We should not despise petitionary prayer; in fact justice demands that we should ask God for things. Jesus encouraged his followers to pray by telling stories of asking and receiving. The long prayer recorded in John 17 is a request by Jesus that His followers may be one – a request that He continues to make in our celebrations of His Eucharist. The Mass (as the liturgy generally) contains much petition, including the 'Our Father' Jesus taught us.

Asking God for things expresses hope and faith. It gives voice to a conviction that God is in charge of all that happens, and to a trust in His loving care. It also expresses love – a love for God, if we pray for His glory; a love for ourselves, when we ask for our needs; a love for others when we seek God's help for them. The dignity of petition is that by it we co-operate with God in the unfolding of His plan! Instead of simply decreeing what should happen, God inspires us to ask Him for various goods, so that they can be given in answer to prayer. Thus He gives a role to His friends in the provision of our needs and in the growth of His Kingdom.

God's answer to our requests is not normally a voice but an event; they are answered by being granted. What of 'unanswered prayer'? We must ask for things honestly and humbly. We ask honestly if we tell God what we want, not what we think we ought to want. (Of course, some of our desires may be sinful, and then we should not ask God for them – but talking to God about them may help to correct them.) We ask humbly if we recognize that He is wiser than we are, and this humility helps us accept the times when there is no answer. A child might ask for a new bicycle when Christmas is near, because the only way she can have one is if the parents give it. But they may have to explain that the family finances do not permit that gift – it is more important to have food and clothing in the new year than a bicycle. The child has to learn to accept that judgement. We, as

God's children, may need to learn from Him what is for the best. The very act of asking implies a submission to His judgement. So when prayer is not answered, we are being asked to 'relativize' the desires we expressed. More important than any particular good is God Himself, and our deepest thirst is for Him. We may need to learn to be content with His friendship and to do without other goods, even though we may not fully understand why it is better for us not to have them all until, in God, we understand all.

Our prayer must therefore be a sharing in the prayer of Christ. At the beginning of His Passion He asked, honestly and humbly, to be spared his suffering, and accepted his need to endure it. His prayer was more than answered in His Resurrection. We – in our much feebler way, and faced with much less anguish – must bring our needs, hopes and desires before our Father, saying with Christ, 'Not my will, but Thine, be done'. Even if our specific requests are not granted, our longings will be more than fulfilled if we can go with Christ to His Father.

In the Mass, we are united with the prayer Christ made on the cross. Christ also prays in His body, the Church, when the *Divine Office* is celebrated, sometimes called *the Liturgy of the Hours*. This is the official prayer of the Church, entrusted to priests and religious, with the rest of the faithful encouraged to participate. It consists of services assigned to particular times of day, chief of which are Lauds (Morning Praise) and Vespers (Evening Prayer). The office is largely made up of Psalms and other scriptural poems. These texts enlarge our concern: if we come to the Office joyful, we may be asked to sing a Psalm of sorrow, or the prayer of one who is persecuted. Then we have to remember that we are part of a body in which some members need forgiveness, some are suffering. If we come to the Office sad, we may be asked to sing a Psalm of rejoicing or victory. Then our hope is renewed, and we are reminded of all those who have already enjoyed God's help. Besides the Psalms, the Office also presents us with Scripture readings, so that we can let God's word sink into us hour by hour, week by week, year by year. We are also offered readings from Christian authors and the Church's teaching authorities, and sing hymns and say prayers composed during the Church's history, so that we can benefit from the wisdom of those who have gone before us in the faith, and their skill may contribute to the beauty of worship.

Ideally, the Office should be celebrated in common, with music and gesture, so that the whole Church is seen to be praying and our minds, voices and bodies are all engaged in worship. The spirit of the Office should inform all our private prayer. It is good to pray at various times of the day and night: when we rise, when we go to bed and as we fall asleep, before and after meals, when we begin some task or it is completed successfully, when we are reminded of someone in need, when we are struck by something of beauty. We can perform our tasks and enjoy our relaxation in a spirit of prayer if we start and end with prayer. All these prayers can be short and simple, spoken aloud or in our hearts; we can use our own words or words composed by others. When performing a mechanical task or on a journey, we can sing a hymn we know, or repeat some formula of prayer over and over. If we can pray simply and spontaneously as the occasion allows, we will become more aware of the presence of God in the whole of our lives, and this will promote a growth in faith and love.

One specially valuable prayer is the *Rosary*, in which the greetings to the Virgin Mary from Luke 1 are repeated over and over, with a request to Mary for her prayers. As the words are repeated, events from the Gospel are put forward for our contemplation. We can simply hold them before our mind's eye, or think over them at length. If we count the prayers on a set of beads, our fingers, voices and minds will all be engaged, as we join Mary who 'kept all these things, pondering them in her heart' (Luke 2:19).

Many people have time they can devote to longer prayer, and are drawn to dwell, in a meditative way, on some text or biblical scene such as the liturgy offers for our contemplation. The slower and more extended private pondering of meditative prayer is one way of allowing God to speak to us through the text or scene, which should also be allowed to inspire praise, thanksgiving and petition. Some people are blessed with a sense of God's closeness and mystery in the course of prayer. But we should not forget that scholarly study of Scripture and theology – if done in faith – is also a form of contemplation, nor that union with the praying Christ can be achieved in many ways. If someone you love is seriously ill, and you call out in panic 'Dear Lord, heal her', you are in union with Christ: you share His love for her, you share something of His prayer, you share something of His anguish.

THE SACRAMENT AND SACRIFICE OF THE HOLY EUCHARIST

At the heart of the Eucharistic celebration are the bread and wine that, by the words of Christ and the invocation of the Holy Spirit, become Christ's Body and Blood . . . The Eucharist is . . . a sacrifice because it *re-presents* (makes present) the sacrifice of the cross, because it is its *memorial* and because it *applies* its fruit . . . In the Eucharist the sacrifice of Christ becomes also the sacrifice of the members of his Body. The lives of the faithful, their praise, sufferings, prayer and work, are united with those of Christ and with his total offering, and so acquire a new value . . . 'by the consecration of the bread and wine there takes place a change of the whole substance of the bread into the substance of the body of Christ our Lord and of the whole substance of the wine into the substance of his blood . . . ' . . . Christ is present whole and entire in each of the species and whole and entire in each of their parts, in such a way that the breaking of the bread does not divide Christ.

(*Catechism* 1333, 1366, 1368, 1376–1377,
quoting the Council of Trent, *Decree on the Eucharist*, 4)

Our consideration of the heart of our liturgy and our Christian life, the Holy Eucharist, may be guided by an anthem St Thomas Aquinas wrote in its honour:

> O sacred Banquet, in which Christ is received,
> the memory of His Passion is renewed,
> the mind is filled with grace,
> and a pledge of future glory is given us.

The Eucharist is a *sacred Banquet*. It is an eating and drinking together, with all that that implies for community rejoicing; but it was never simply a shared meal, but always a ritual, full of meaning, and the source of meaning for the lives of those who celebrate it. Its sacredness does not mean that the world outside the Mass is outside the sphere of God's love. Rather, the natural goods God makes must be lifted up to the divine level by priestly action. The priestly action of God's Son was to take our human nature, and in it to offer Himself and go into glory. The priestly action of God's people is to make all of their life and work into an offering, and to follow Christ into glory. Christ's priestly action inspires His people's priestly action through the priestly action of the Eucharist, in which the bread and wine we have made are taken up by Christ so that we may be drawn into His offering and His body, and pointed forward to a world glorified.

The Western Church uses a ritual form of bread for the Eucharist, unleavened bread, such as the Jews use for the Passover. This reminds us that Christ is our Passover, and that in the Eucharist we enter into the great events of salvation, as the Passover enabled the Jews to experience the deliverance from Egypt.

In the Eucharist, *Christ is received*. The Church takes literally what Jesus said: 'This is my body . . . This is the cup of my blood.' By God's power, the bread and wine become the body and blood of Christ. Thus the Holy Eucharist is an example of the 'homeliness' of God. God has given Himself to us, in the Person of the Word, in the Incarnation. The Word made flesh gave Himself as fully as possible, to the extent of dying on the cross. And He continues to give Himself as fully as possible, by being with us in the Eucharist, by being received in the Eucharist. None of this was strictly necessary; it demonstrates the limitless generosity of God, and encourages us to hope for God's final self-giving, the beatific vision.

After the consecration, the Sacrament is no longer literally bread and wine even though, because Jesus spoke of Himself as the Bread of Life, the liturgy can speak of 'the holy Bread of life eternal and the Cup of unending salvation' (Roman Canon). We often refer to the Sacrament in the form of bread as the *host*, from the Latin word for sacrifice; and as a way of expressing the greatness of this Sacrament in which Christ is truly present, we sometimes call it the *Blessed Sacrament*. (The word 'blessed' in this phrase is pronounced with two syllables.)

The Fathers of the Church believed in, and taught, the change of bread and wine into the body and blood of Christ. Recognizing the flesh of the divine Word as life-giving, they saw how precious is the chance to receive it. From the twelfth century the term *transubstantiation* came to be used for the change of bread and wine into Christ's body and blood, and St Thomas explored what it might mean in a particularly subtle way. We can distinguish between what something is (its *sub-*

stance) and its properties. For there are times when a change in properties does not involve a change in what something is, and vice versa. A tree may grow in size, and change colour with the seasons, while it remains the same tree. If it is burned, however, it becomes a different thing. When a dog dies, it becomes something else, a corpse, but some of its properties, such as the colour of its coat, persist for a time. In the case of the Holy Eucharist, *what* is present changes: the bread becomes the body of Christ, the wine becomes His blood. But none of the properties changes: the size, taste, colour, position, nourishing or intoxicating power, and so on, of the bread and wine, remain. And they are *not* the size, taste, colour, position, nourishing or intoxicating power of the body and blood of Christ; rather, we claim that 'beneath' all these properties Christ is present. And this is not a contradiction in terms, since substance and properties are logically distinct.

Just as we can see that the doctrines of the Trinity and the Incarnation are not logically impossible, while they remain mysteries, so Christ's presence in the Holy Eucharist remains a mystery, it is not explained away. It cannot be fitted into any of the types of change we are used to, for only in the case of the Eucharist are the properties we observe not those of the substance beneath them. If I ferment five gallons of grape juice I obtain five gallons of wine. The same amount of 'stuff' is present, though its chemical structure has been altered. Something new has come to exist, but there is an underlying continuity. If I consecrate a quarter of a pint of wine, however, I do *not* get a quarter of a pint of Christ's blood. I get the whole of Christ's blood – and each person who drinks from the chalice receives the whole of Christ's blood, indeed, *the whole Christ*. This change is more radical than any natural change; it relies on the creative power of God. Natural causes can change the structures of things; God can work on the whole being of things. The whole being of the wine becomes the whole being of Christ's blood, and His blood is wholly present beneath every part of what is in the chalice.

We must not think of the properties of bread and wine as merely a convenient disguise for Christ. True, He comes to us 'veiled' because we are on pilgrimage and cannot see Him in His glory, but the appearances of bread and wine do *reveal* Him.

They show us Christ coming to us as food for the journey, as our source of unity, as the cause of our joy. The properties of the bread and wine are the signs of Christ who is present beneath them, and of His work.[8]

The Christ who is present in the Eucharist is the risen Christ. Raised from the dead, He cannot suffer. Therefore His body cannot be found without His blood, or His soul – and never was it without His godhead, for it is the body of the divine Word. The power in Christ's words – 'This is my body' – make His body present beneath the appearances of bread; but where His body is, there the whole Christ is. So in the Host we receive the whole Christ, body, blood, soul and godhead; and the same is true when we drink from the chalice.

Although the whole Christ is present under the appearance of bread and under the appearance of wine, it is essential that at every Mass both should be consecrated and both received, so that the symbolism of the Eucharist may be complete. It is not necessary that *all* who receive Communion should receive under both forms. For a long time only the celebrating priest received from the chalice in the Western Church; for convenience and safety others received under the form of bread alone. People allergic to gluten have been allowed to receive only from the chalice. If you receive under one form only, you receive the whole Christ, you receive all the grace He comes to give. Nowadays, in many places, the congregation are invited to receive under both forms, at least on some occasions, so that the richer symbolism may inspire deeper devotion.

Communion is taken to the sick and housebound under the form of bread, so Hosts are reserved after Mass in a special safe, called the *tabernacle*. Because Christ is present beneath the appearances of bread and wine, the Blessed Sacrament may and should be adored. When we worship it, we are worshipping Jesus. In the course of the Mass, the priest genuflects (bends the knee) to the Sacrament, and we genuflect to the Blessed Sacrament in the tabernacle on entering and leaving Church. It is good to pray before the tabernacle. Sometimes special services are held in honour of Christ's presence in the Sacrament. It may be carried in procession, or placed in a 'monstrance' that holds it up so that it may be seen and adored. After a period of 'exposition', it may be raised in blessing over the people present – this is called *Benediction*. Of course, Jesus is present in the Blessed Sacrament so that we may receive Him in Holy Communion, but these services of adoration remind us who it is that we receive. Our guest is God!

Christ's presence in the Sacrament is brought about automatically whenever one who has been ordained priest recites Christ's words over wheat bread and grape wine, within a rite that makes clear his intention to do what Christ told His disciples to do. The personal holiness of the priest is irrelevant, since the power at work is Christ's, not his. However, Jesus is present and is received, not just to be with us but to enrich us with His grace. *The purpose of the Sacrament is to build us up into the body of Christ*, to make us live as His members with greater love and vitality. This ultimate effect of the Eucharist is not achieved automatically, magically; it depends on the receptivity of the communicant. One who comes to Communion with great devotion is more open to Jesus' influence than one who comes inattentively or to please others. One who is in a state of mortal sin should not come at all, until the sin has been repented of and (if at all possible) confessed. If, say, I have defrauded an elderly widow of her savings, and come to Mass enjoying the thought of what I can buy with the money, I do not want to be built up in love. If I were to receive Communion, I would be guilty of hypocrisy and insult, for I would be expressing a desire for charity and unity deceitfully.

In the Eucharist, *the memory of Christ's Passion is renewed*. The Sacrament looks back to all the great mysteries of Jesus. His dwelling in our midst is perpetuated. The risen Christ is among us, who was recognized in the breaking of bread by two disciples on Easter Sunday evening. But above all His Passion is commemorated. The consecration first of bread and then of wine is a symbol of the giving of His body and the shedding of His blood. It is more than a symbol: just as Jesus who once gave Himself is present in the Eucharist, so the power of His self-giving is present in the Eucharist. It is a *sacrifice*. The one, perfect sacrifice is Jesus' self-giving on the cross: the Eucharist is not a substitute for that, nor does it work alongside it; it is a kind of extension of it. Jesus does not die again in the Mass, but the powerful, sacred action accomplished 2,000 years ago is symbolized and mystically made present. Therefore the Old Testament sacrifices, which prophesied Christ's sacrifice, particularly the communion sacrifices and the Passover, also prophesied the Holy Eucharist.

Christ's sacrifice on the cross was the channel of God's saving power, and the Eucharist channels that power further. Those who receive Communion with devotion grow in grace. All who are present at Mass, who have brought their efforts and sufferings to unite them to Christ's self-giving, draw strength to live out their share in His priestly action. Official prayers are spoken at Mass for the Church, her ministers, and various intentions; sometimes spontaneous prayers may be spoken aloud; and all those present will have their private desires. The power of Christ's Passion flows to all those prayed for. When a priest consecrates the Eucharist, and so represents Christ's sacrifice, he is entitled to apply the power of that sacrifice to some particular need. People often ask priests to *offer Mass* for their intentions, such as the cure for someone who is sick, or the eternal rest of someone who has died and may be in Purgatory. On such occasions they usually make an offering to the Church (a 'stipend') so as to support the celebration of the Mass and make a gesture of solidarity with Christ's self-giving.

In the Eucharist, *the mind is filled with grace.* Jesus comes to us under the form of food because He comes to us as our Food. Our share in the divine life flows to us through the humanity of Jesus, and is nourished by the Holy Eucharist in which Jesus' humanity is symbolized and present. By the Eucharist we are strengthened to 'imitate what we celebrate', we are given power to model our lives on Christ's sacrifice which we commemorate. Jesus' body was formed by the Holy Spirit in Mary's womb, and through the offering of that body the Holy Spirit was made available to us. Therefore some Eucharistic Prayers invoke the Holy Spirit upon the bread and wine that they may become Christ's body and blood, and after the consecration they pray that 'we who are nourished by [Jesus'] body and blood may be filled with His Holy Spirit, and become one body, one spirit in Christ'. We receive Jesus, who gave us the Holy Spirit, so that He may give us the Holy Spirit.

We receive the Eucharist to 'become one body, one spirit in Christ', for Jesus comes to us to build us up into His body, His people. The ultimate goal of the Sacrament is to create the 'mystical body of Christ', the Church herself. The community of the Church is symbolized by the rite of the Eucharist: grains of wheat and grapes are brought together to make the bread and wine used, and the sharing of food and drink is an important human way of building up community, which God employs as an effective sign of His work building up His people. So St Augustine hails the Eucharist: 'O sacrament of love, O sign of unity, O bond of charity!' (*On John's Gospel* 26, 6, 13).

In the Eucharist, *a pledge of future glory is given us*. The Bible shows us the Kingdom under the images of a great feast and banquet, the 'marriage supper of the Lamb'. Of this the Eucharist is a symbol, and more than a symbol. It gives us the power to be part of that great feast, for the body and blood of Jesus are 'the medicine of immortality' – 'He who eats my flesh and drinks my blood has eternal life, and I will raise him up at the last day . . . he who eats me will live because of me . . . he who eats this bread will live for ever' (John 6:54–58). In the Kingdom, we will be 'fed', made alive, by Jesus with the vision of His Father, and we share Their joy, that is, Their Spirit. So Jesus comes to us now under the appearances of bread, which is food and (for the Jews of His time) a symbol of knowledge, and of wine, a source of joy.

It was long the custom at Mass for everyone to face east for the main prayers, as an expression of longing for Christ's coming in glory, of which the rising of the Sun is an image, and the Mass a foretaste. In the revised rite of Mass, our looking forward to Jesus' coming in glory has been made more explicit in the prayers. We are asked to abstain from food and drink (except water) for at least an hour before receiving Holy Communion, not because there is something 'unclean' about normal food, but because this deliberate turning from the food that nourishes this life to the Food of eternal life is a sign of our hope for the Kingdom. Those who are dying are encouraged to receive Holy Communion, and then it is called *Viaticum*, food for the journey, since the risen Jesus comes to them to help them on the most crucial step of their pilgrimage to the feast of the Kingdom.

NOTES

1 For a time the last words of the Mass were: *Ite, missa est. Deo gratias* ('Go, the congregation is sent forth. Thanks be to God'). Those are again the last words of Mass celebrated in Latin, now

that the rite has been revised. The word *missa* came, rather oddly, to be used as a name for the service.

2 See Chapter 11 for an explanation of 'the Eastern Churches'.

3 This detail is only preserved in one account of the Last Supper, in Luke 22:17, since Jesus gave no new significance to the cup before the meal.

4 The exact form of words differs from one account to another. See Matthew 26:26–29, Mark 14:22–25, Luke 22:14–20 and 1 Corinthians 11:23–26. It may be that some of the formulae used in different areas in the early Church go back by oral tradition to the words Jesus actually used, since the Eucharist was being celebrated before those four accounts were written down.

5 From the Roman Missal, ICEL translation.

6 In Britain, the 'Holydays of Obligation' are: Christmas Day (25 December); the Epiphany (6 January); the Ascension (40 days after Easter); Corpus Christi (second Thursday after Pentecost); Sts Peter and Paul (29 June); the Assumption (15 August); All Saints (1 November).

In Scotland, the Epiphany and Corpus Christi are always transferred to the nearest Sunday. When a Holyday of Obligation falls on a Saturday or Monday, special rules apply (except in the case of Christmas Day).

7 'Scientific' in the sense in which history and similar 'arts' subjects can be called 'scientific'.

8 Because the appearances of bread and wine have to reveal Christ to human beings, He remains present as long as they remain accessible to average human senses. The particles that may fly off when the Host is broken, too small for the eye to tell whether they are bread or dust, and the stain that may be left on the cloth when the chalice is wiped, are not the body and blood of Christ. We must, of course, collect and consume any fragments of the Host; and out of reverence for the Sacrament, we collect and consume what we can even of the minute particles.

CHAPTER 9

SHARING CHRIST'S PRIESTHOOD
AND MINISTRY

OUR NEED FOR SACRAMENTS

The seven sacraments touch all the stages and all the important
moments of Christian life: they give birth and increase, healing
and mission . . . Since Pentecost, it is through the sacramental
signs of his Church that the Holy Spirit carries on the work of
sanctification. The sacraments of the Church do not abolish but
purify and integrate all the richness of the signs and symbols of
the cosmos and of social life. Further, they fulfil the types and
figures of the Old Covenant, signify and make actively present
the salvation wrought by Christ, and prefigure and anticipate the
glory of heaven.

(Catechism 1210, 1152)

THE Holy Eucharist is the greatest of the seven *sacraments*.
They resemble each other in some ways, and differ in
others. They all show us Christ's saving work, and channel His
grace and strength to those who receive them; but since only the
Eucharist brings the effects of His sacrifice to those for whom it
is offered as well as to those who receive it, it alone is both
sacrament and sacrifice.

As the Eucharist places the pattern of Christ's self-giving on
our lives, helping us to imitate what we celebrate, so the other
sacraments shape our lives; they help us to grow into Christ and
journey to His Kingdom. In fact, a parallel can be drawn
between the natural course of human life and the pattern
marked out by the sacraments. We begin our life in human
society by being born, and we come to birth as Christians by
Baptism, in which God first plants His life in us. This is the
most essential of the sacraments, while the Eucharist is the
greatest. In many societies there is a ritual of coming-of-age,

and we are brought to maturity as Christians by Confirmation. Human life is preserved, and society cemented, by eating and drinking, and our life as Christians is nourished, our community is strengthened, by the Holy Eucharist. Natural human society is held together at the level of the family by marriage and at the level of the state by forms of leadership, and the Christian community is built by marriage – given a new dignity in Christ – and by the ministerial priesthood. Human life is damaged by the physical disorder of sickness, and by moral and psychological disorders. There is a sacramental remedy for sickness, the Anointing of the Sick, which aims to restore the sick to the exercise of their activities in the Church; and there is a sacramental remedy for sin, Reconciliation, which restores the life of grace when it has been lost. (These two sacraments will be dealt with in the next chapter.) Our natural life comes to an end at death, but no sacrament corresponds to this, for our Christian life does not end. Rather, all the sacraments point us forward in hope to the greater flourishing of our Christian lives in God's Kingdom.

All created things are signs of God's wisdom, beauty and goodness. By contemplating the world around us we can come to know its Creator. But we would have no idea of His plan of salvation unless He were to show us what He is doing for us, and for that He must choose special signs by which to communicate with us. The basic sign is Christ Himself, the Word made flesh, through whom the Father has spoken to us; and because His Word is powerful to fulfil itself, Jesus' life, death and Resurrection contain the power to save. If people are to be brought into contact with God's Word, by the response of faith, they must 'overhear' what was spoken into our world 2,000 years ago.

The people of the Old Testament saw Christ's saving work, as it was prefigured in the rituals God gave them, the sacrifices and sacraments of the Old Law. So they could be saved by their faith in the Christ promised. The Bible shows us friends of God who lived before He gave a Law, such as Noah, who spontaneously offered Him sacrifice. Thomas Aquinas suggests that such people chose their own sacraments by which Christ's saving work could be (if obscurely) signified; and we might suggest that Christ's work can still be obscurely signified in the rites of peoples to whom the Law and the Gospel have not yet come.[1] God may speak to people in the depths of their hearts and through the wisdom of their society.

We who follow Christ overhear the divine Word more clearly, in the Scriptures, in which He speaks to us, and – in a specially rich way – in the sacraments He left us. They suit our needs. For we communicate with each other by word and gesture, and affect each other by so doing. The sacraments are 'words and gestures' of God, by which He communicates with us and graces us. It is not that God speaks afresh every time a sacrament is celebrated; we overhear God's definitive Word that was spoken into this world when the Son came among us, and the sacraments have saving power because the Word's power to fulfil itself is at work in them. So the sacraments *effect what they signify*: through them, God shows us what He is doing, and does what He shows us. As an analogy, consider how you write. The most effective way is to grasp a pen with your hand. The hand is adapted for grasping, and the pen for writing – they are suitable tools, even though neither could work by itself, for the power to write is yours. God channels His grace to us through the best 'tools': through the human life, death and Resurrection of Christ (joined to God in the Incarnation as the hand is to the writer); and from thence through the sacraments (taken up from outside as the writer takes up the pen).

In human relationships, actions speak louder than words. When God communicates with us, He does so by actions whose meaning cannot fully be put into words, and in particular by Jesus' death on the cross. So it should not surprise us to find Him communicating with us through simple yet profound rituals. There is, of course, a human delight in ritual, which God draws on in the sacraments. The Church also draws on it, to enrich her liturgy with what are called *sacramentals*. For example, on 2 February, in memory of the Presentation of Jesus in the temple, when Simeon recognized Him as the Light to enlighten the nations, we have a procession with lighted candles; and on Palm Sunday we commemorate Jesus' triumphal entry into Jerusalem by a procession with palm branches. Many of the sacramentals can be seen as 'acted out prayers'. When we use holy water to bless ourselves or our homes, we are asking God to renew within us the grace of Baptism, and to cleanse and protect us from sin. Sacramentals can be used to bring reminders of God's care into the details of our lives.

Homes and boats, schools and libraries, foodstuffs and medi-
cines may all be blessed, and then the Church's official prayer
accompanies our use of them. When we keep images of Christ
and his saints by us, we are moved to imitate their lives and
their holiness, and to seek their intercession. But while the
sacramentals are words of the Church, the sacraments are, at
root, words of God Himself, and so are words of special power.

The use of material things – bread and wine, water and oil –
as instruments of grace reminds us of the goodness of creation.
When we see God's saving work revealed through material
signs, we are encouraged to see His beauty revealed in the world
at large. Because of sin, we can be enslaved to material things,
and our relationships can be marred by cruelty and exploitation. The use of material things, and of the ministry of human
beings, as means of grace, proclaims God's healing work. So the
sacraments shape and energize our Christian lives; they open
our eyes to see God's presence everywhere; and, as medicine for
a world from which we try to exclude God, they bring healing.

BAPTISM – OUR NEW CREATION

Through Baptism we are freed from sin and reborn as sons of
God; we become members of Christ, are incorporated into the
Church and made sharers in her mission . . . The sheer
gratuitousness of the gift of salvation is particularly manifest in
infant Baptism . . . The baptized . . . share in the priesthood of
Christ, in his prophetic and royal mission.

                    (*Catechism* 1213, 1250, 1268)

Baptism is a ritual washing. Besides the ritual washings
prescribed by the Old Testament, Jewish practice employed
others, and converts to Judaism were baptized (men also being
circumcised). Jesus' cousin, John the Baptist, proclaimed that
the Messiah was imminent, and called people to be baptized
as a sign of repentance before the judgement began. In fact
the judgement began with Jesus sharing baptism with the
sinners, as it was to come to a climax at His crucifixion between
two bandits. Jesus and His disciples seem to have baptized in
the course of His ministry; certainly after Pentecost people
became His disciples by Baptism, in obedience to His command: 'make disciples of all nations, baptizing them in the
name of the Father, and of the Son and of the Holy Spirit' (John

3:22; 4:1–2; Matthew 28:19). For some time, it seems, the
words of Baptism were in the form of questions: 'Do you
believe in God the Father . . . ?' 'I believe.' 'Do you believe in
Christ Jesus, the Son of God . . . ?' 'I believe.' 'Do you believe
in the Holy Spirit in the holy Church . . . ?' 'I believe.' At each
'I believe' the candidate was immersed in water.[2] The questions
came to be asked before the actual rite of Baptism, so the form
of Baptism now is: 'I baptize you in the name of the Father, and
of the Son, and of the Holy Spirit.' As the minister says this, he
(or she) pours water over the candidate's head, or immerses the
candidate in water, three times (once would be valid). Baptism
is normally celebrated by a bishop, priest or deacon, accompa-
nied with explanatory ceremonies. In an emergency, such as
when a baby is in danger of death, it may be performed simply,
by pouring water and reciting the form of words given above;
and, because of its urgency, it may be performed by any man or
woman, Christian or not.

We read in the Acts of the Apostles (16:33) of a convert being
baptized 'with all his household'. It often happened in the early
Church that children were baptized. If they were too young to
answer for themselves, adults answered for them. Later it
became the custom to defer Baptism until the risk of serious
post-baptismal sins had cooled off,[3] but the Church soon
reverted to the custom of baptizing infants whose parents were
to bring them up as Christians. This makes it clear that the
initiative is always God's when we come to faith. Besides
drawing adults to Himself, He can plant His life in children,
with the virtues of faith, hope and charity latent in their minds
and wills.

As a washing, Baptism speaks of the cleansing away of sin.
But we have seen that the forgiveness of sins is the same as the
coming of grace, in which God's love turns us back to Him and
gives us strength to live as His children. So Baptism is the
means by which God first plants His life in us, it is when we are
created anew, born again, made divine. This is symbolized by
the water, for water brings life in the desert, water flows at
birth. The biblical story shows God creating the world out of a
watery chaos. Water flowed from Christ's side after He had died
for the life of the Church, as water flowed from the Temple in
Ezekiel's vision and became a river of life (John 19:34; Ezekiel
47:1–12). When we are baptized, we 'go down into the Jordan'

with Christ at His Baptism, and overhear the Father's voice: 'Thou art my beloved son' (Mark 1:11). We are born as God's children, sharing the sonship of Christ, adopted in Him. The Holy Spirit who was then seen as a dove comes to us in Baptism, enabling us to live as the Father's children.

Water can also cause death. St Paul teaches that Baptism is a dying with Christ; we are buried with Him (Romans 6:3–4). This is most clearly seen if Baptism is performed by immersion, for going under the water is a symbolic burial. We die to sin so that we can live a new and richer life, and our new life is a share in Christ's Resurrection. When we go through the water, therefore, we begin to share in Christ's journey through death to new life; and we live out our Baptism by continuing to put sin to death and letting the divine life shape our behaviour, so that we go forward in the strength of our Baptism until we fully share in Christ's Resurrection. The favoured time for adult Baptism is during the Easter Vigil on the night of the Resurrection. At that Vigil, Exodus 14:15 – 15:1 is read, which tells how the people of Israel escaped from the oppression of Egypt through the Red Sea. The Bible shows them being formed as God's people in the course of their journey through the wilderness, during which they were fed with miraculous bread, 'Manna', until they reached the promised land. Christians are set free from the oppression of sin to be God's pilgrim people by the waters of Baptism, which marks the beginning of our journey to the Kingdom. In the course of that journey we are formed into Christ's members by reading the Scriptures and by being fed with the supernatural food of the Eucharist.

The Church recognizes the Baptism of all Christians, Catholic or not. In the early Church, some theologians thought there could be no true Baptism outside the Catholic Church, but that idea was rejected since man-made divisions cannot nullify the promise Christ has attached to the rite. This implied there is an element in Baptism independent of whether the recipient has charity, since it was difficult then to recognise the good faith of non-Catholic Christians, and schism is contrary to charity. In Holy Communion, those with and those without charity both receive Christ's body and blood; in Baptism, the element independent of charity is what we call *character*, the Greek word for the impression made by a seal. By Baptism we are stamped as belonging to Christ, and that is irrevocable. Whenever anyone is baptized, this character or status is imparted. They must, of course, come to faith: a baby is baptized in the faith of its mother the Church, but an adult must give a sign of faith. If you poured water on a protesting adult who did not want to accept the faith, it would be no Baptism at all.

There is also an element in Baptism which is dependent on whether the recipient comes to have charity, and this is the new life of grace itself. Our share in God's life, which works through charity, is as a rule given us in Baptism. But it is possible to resist grace and refuse to love. Someone who does not want to be built up in love may receive Christ's body in Holy Communion, the Sacrament of love, but to no benefit. An adult who comes to faith and seeks Baptism, but is secretly determined to persist in some serious sin, is truly baptized, but does not yet have the life of grace. This only flows through when he repents of his sin. Conversely, this element of Baptism may be shared by one who has not yet received the sacrament and its character. Someone who desires Baptism has already laid hold on a share in this life by means of this desire which God has inspired, and Baptism will strengthen this share in the divine life. This fact does not make Baptism irrelevant, just as the joy of courtship does not make marriage unnecessary.

Baptismal character, our being stamped as belonging to Christ, is a sharing in His priesthood. It entitles us to take part in the Eucharistic sacrifice by receiving Holy Communion, and it commits us to live out Christ's sacrifice in our daily lives by imitating His self-giving love. It makes our prayer a sharing in Christ's prayer, it makes our struggle for justice in our lives and relationships a sharing in His Passion.

Baptism is given us as the way to become God's children. We must give it to our own children, as God's ministers, and offer it to non-Christians as we preach the Gospel to them. To reject Baptism is to reject God's offer of salvation, but that warning is not heard by those who do not hear the Gospel, so (as suggested above) such people may perhaps belong to Christ as Noah did, and are not automatically to be seen as having rejected God. As regards children who die without Baptism, we do not know of any way in which God's life has been brought to them, a life which original sin means we lack unless it is brought to us. Many theologians supposed that such children end up in a state called *Limbo*,[4] a state of perfect *natural* happiness, in which they will suffer no pain or distress, and will know about God and His wisdom, but not know Him by the beatific vision. Nowadays many prefer to be agnostic on the issue, and hope that God brings such children to a supernatural joy by ways we do not need to be told.

CONFIRMATION, THE GIFT OF THE SPIRIT'S STRENGTH

> . . . the effect of the sacrament of Confirmation is the full outpouring of the Holy Spirit as was once granted to the apostles on the day of Pentecost . . . the 'character' [it imprints] . . . is the sign that Jesus Christ has marked a Christian with the seal of his Spirit by clothing him with power from on high that he may be his witness. This 'character' perfects the common priesthood of the faithful, received in Baptism . . .
>
> (*Catechism* 1302, 1304–1305)

Before His ascension, Jesus promised His disciples they would be clothed with power from on high, and this promise was fulfilled on the day of Pentecost by the outpouring of the Spirit Jesus had won for us. The Spirit was visibly at work in the early Church by various signs that helped her grow at that critical stage in her history. In Acts 8:14–17 we read how, when Baptism was given by ministers other than the Apostles, and no visible signs of the Spirit occurred, the Apostles came to lay hands on the new Christians so that they might receive the Spirit. After a couple of centuries, we find a similar pattern being followed in the Church's rites of initiation. On Easter night, Baptism was administered to new Christians in a baptistery attached to the cathedral, often by a priest rather than by the bishop; but it was followed by an anointing with oil, performed by the bishop as he invoked the Holy Spirit on the newly-baptized, who would then receive their white garments and enter the cathedral for their first Holy Communion. We may say, then, that *Confirmation* is the rite in which the bishop, as successor of the Apostles, gives the Holy Spirit to those who have been baptized but need to be further strengthened. Because, after the Church's early years, the gifts of the Holy Spirit have not often been spectacular – we saw in Chapter 4 that wisdom is one of the greatest, and charity the chief – the outward sign of oil was adopted so that the Spirit's coming might be made visible. Through the sacrament of Confirmation, Pentecost is prolonged throughout the Church's history.

In the Eastern Churches, it remained usual to give Confirmation immediately after Baptism, so when babies are baptized they are at once anointed by the priest with *Chrism*, a perfumed oil the bishop has consecrated. In the West it remained usual for the bishop to confirm, so children who have been baptized are confirmed nearer adult life, in the course of the bishop's visit; but on occasion Confirmation is administered by a priest. The bishop is involved, even when a priest confirms, because only he can consecrate the Chrism, which he does at Mass on Maundy Thursday. In the current Western rite, the bishop or priest stretches his hands over the candidates, and prays for them to receive the Holy Spirit with His gifts; then he anoints each candidate on the forehead with Chrism, saying: 'Be sealed with the Gift of the Holy Spirit'.

Because it is usually older children or young adults who are confirmed in Western practice, it is sometimes thought that the name 'Confirmation' refers to their decision to persevere in the Christian faith; that is, in this rite they confirm the profession of faith made by others on their behalf when they were baptized. In fact, however, the Latin word *confirmatio* means 'strengthening', 'encouraging'; it is the sacrament in which the Holy Spirit strengthens us, comes as the Friend who is to encourage us to persevere in the faith. The work is His, not ours. In Baptism, God has marked us as His own, and a decision for or against the faith made in later life is not neutral: perseverance in the faith is expected of us, since we should be loyal to the God who has made us His friends, and abandoning the faith is precisely that, a disloyalty to God. So, whether it is received at once or years later, Confirmation is the appropriate sequel to Baptism, just as coming of age is the natural sequel to human birth.

The Holy Spirit who comes to us in Baptism comes again with new power in Confirmation, to bring us to maturity in Christ. We are *irrevocably sealed* again, with the duty to live as mature Christians, faithful to the gifts we have been given. Having been given the strength to live as God's children, free from sin, we are given further strength to share in the ministry of Christ. That is why we are anointed with oil called Chrism, for the Spirit who came visibly on Jesus at His Baptism – the beginning of His public ministry – to reveal Him as the Christ, the Lord's Anointed, comes on us to give us a share in His anointing and a share in His public ministry. We are given a share in Christ's roles as Priest, Prophet and King. We are called as priests to make our lives into a service of God, to bring the whole world before God by praising Him on its behalf, and to bring His blessing on the world by our peace-making. As prophets we are called to speak God's truth as His witnesses, and to speak for the poor and oppressed. As sharers in Christ's kingly role we are called to defeat evil and promote justice – sometimes this means sharing his cross – and to bring people into His Kingdom. The Western custom of giving Confirmation around the beginning of adult life reminds us that this sacrament gives us a more adult, public share in Christ's priesthood. It is not inappropriate for people to be drawn to welcome this gift at an age when they are becoming aware of their need for it.

As well as looking back to the ministry of the Messiah and to the day of Pentecost, and as well as showing us the strength and dignity the Spirit gives us now – for oil is a traditional symbol of strength and dignity – Confirmation also points us forward to the Kingdom in which we shall share the Holy Spirit of joy, and wear a robe of glory as a reward for the faithful use of God's gifts.

THE MINISTERIAL PRIESTHOOD

The ordained ministry or *ministerial* priesthood is at the service of the baptismal priesthood. The ordained priesthood guarantees that it really is Christ who acts in the sacraments through the Holy Spirit for the Church. The saving mission entrusted by the Father to his incarnate Son was committed to the apostles and through them to their successors: they receive the Spirit of Jesus to act in his name and in his person. The ordained minister is the sacramental bond that ties the liturgical action to what the apostles said and did and, through them, to the words and actions of Christ, the source and foundation of the sacraments . . . the one priesthood of Christ . . . is made present through the ministerial priesthood without diminishing the uniqueness of Christ's priesthood . . . Through the ordained ministry, especially that of bishops and priests, the presence of Christ as

head of the Church is made visible in the midst of the
community of believers.

(Catechism 1120, 1545, 1549)

Jesus chose twelve Apostles to lead the community of His
followers, for the old Israel was notionally made up of twelve
tribes. Other men, like the Apostles Matthias (the replacement
for Judas) and Paul, and some of Jesus' relatives, were also
recognized or appointed to share in the leadership of the early
Church. That foundational body enjoyed special authority.
When it was being decided which writings belong in the New
Testament, it was held that they must have apostolic authority
behind them; it is from the Apostles that the Church's tradition
has come down; it is with the close of their generation that
revelation ceased. But as the Church spread, and leaders were
needed in more and more places, the Apostles and their
colleagues passed on a share in their authority by the laying on
of hands. It may be that the precise structure of the Church's
leadership crystallized during an 'embryonic period', rather as
the human body has an embryonic period after which its structure is comparatively fixed. Certainly the Church emerged from
the apostolic period with a three-fold ministry, which can be
seen forming in the New Testament itself. This 'leadership
structure' has been perpetuated in unbroken succession by the
sacrament of Orders, which involves the laying on of hands. The
three Orders received the Greek names *episkopoi, presbyteroi*
and *diakonoi*, which literally mean 'overseers', 'elders' and
'servers', and give us the words 'bishops', 'priests' and 'deacons'. These titles were already used for various officials in pagan
cultic guilds, but as they were the most colourless of the titles in
use they were the most adaptable to a Christian interpretation,
rather as the word *agapē* was the most adaptable word for love.

The pagan, sacrificing priests were called, in Greek, *hiereis*
(the English word 'priest', derived from *presbyteros*, is also used
to translate *hiereus*); but our sacrifice is not like theirs. The
Jewish priests who offered sacrifice in the Temple in Jerusalem
are also called *hiereis* in the New Testament, but their sacrifices
were rendered out-of-date by Jesus' death. Therefore the word
hiereis was not used for Christian ministers, though the New
Testament does use it and related words for Jesus and the whole
Christian people, since Jesus' death fulfilled the Jewish rites in

an unexpected way, and we share in His sacrifice by imitating His self-giving.

We need to be encouraged by our leaders to imitate Jesus; we need to be built up into a priestly people by the power of His sacrifice being brought home to us in our own place and time. This is done most richly by the sacraments, especially the Eucharist. Because of its necessity, Baptism may be validly administered by anyone; and the bride and groom administer the sacrament of Marriage to each other. But in the case of the other sacraments, the power of the sacrifice of Christ our Head is brought to us through the ministry of bishops and priests ordained to lead in the Church. This means that the sacraments have come down to us from Christ Himself, via the Apostles, through a succession of ministers that can be traced back through history. The sacrament of Orders points us back to Christ and the men He gathered round Himself and sent out with authority.

Those who are ordained, then, are *stamped with a new share in Christ's priesthood*, so that His own ministry by which He builds up His Church may be kept alive in her through the ages. Bishops and priests do not offer new sacrifices in their own right; they minister Christ's one sacrifice. Once the difference between Christian and pagan worship was made clear, and once the all-sufficiency of Christ's sacrifice compared with the Jewish sacrifices was made clear, the Church was free to apply the word *hiereus* (*sacerdos* in Latin) to the Christian minister. The three-fold Old Testament priesthood – High Priest, priests and Levites – was then seen as foreshadowing the Christian ministry of bishop, priests and deacons. It was recognized that, because Christian priests act *in persona Christi* (in Christ's role), they offer sacrifice when celebrating the Eucharist, in that through their action Christ perpetuates His one sacrifice so that His people may enter into it and its power may be channelled to those who need it.

The role of ordained ministers in the sacraments goes with their role as leaders, which involves guiding and teaching. For in their exercise of both roles Christ is at work building up His body through those who share His ministry. And, because they are leaders, bishops and priests can be seen as acting on behalf of the Church, Christ's body, when they celebrate the sacraments in which He is at work in His members. The sacrament of Orders brings help to bishops, priests and deacons so that their lives can be worthy of their ministry. But the most essential elements in this ministry – the celebration of true sacraments and the preservation of the true faith – do not depend on whether they use this help. The way in which Christ can build up His people even through unworthy ministers shows us the power of His grace to overcome sin, and points us forward to the Kingdom in which we will reflect God's glory to each other without obscuring stain.

The bishop presides over an area, called a *diocese*, as a successor of the Apostles. Many priests are deputed by bishops to preside over smaller areas, called *parishes* (not all priests are called upon to carry out various forms of pastoral care and to preach; some exercise their priesthood in enclosed monasteries, by praying and offering Mass for the good of the whole Church). When the bishop celebrates Mass, assisted by priests, deacons and representatives of various groups in the diocese, the local Church is most clearly made visible sacramentally. When priests 'concelebrate' with the bishop or as a body of priests, reciting together Christ's words over the bread and wine, it is seen that one priesthood, namely Christ's, is exercised by them.

As individuals, as local groups and, especially, as a body whose focus of unity is the Bishop of Rome, the bishops continue the apostolic work of proclaiming the Gospel by preaching the truth and refuting error. As the 'High Priest' of his diocese, the bishop ministers the grace of Christ, the true High Priest, notably through the sacraments that most build up the structure of the body of Christ, Confirmation and Orders. When a new bishop is to be consecrated, several bishops of the area confer the sacrament together; when priests are ordained, the local priests join the bishop in laying hands on the new priests. The Pope, as Bishop of Rome, is elected by the cardinals, who are the bishops of the suburbs of Rome and the 'honorary clergy' of her older churches. So as to ensure the Church's independence of civil rulers, the popes have repeatedly taken to themselves the responsibility of appointing other bishops; this manifests their care for the universal Church and their role as guardian of the communion of the bishops.

Deacons share in Christ's role as Servant of His bride, the Church, and so are ordained to carry out various forms of administrative and pastoral care. At Mass, the deacon reads the Gospel and assists the priest or bishop at the altar, and he may preach; he may baptize, preside at weddings, conduct funerals and lead some forms of worship, giving a blessing at the end.

Besides the three Orders of bishops, priests and deacons, the Church has had, and has, other orders and ministries, and the authority of the bishops has been and is shared in more complicated ways than suggested above. For example, abbots and heads of certain religious orders take part in Ecumenical Councils; abbesses have sometimes had significant power; and we hear of deaconesses in the early Church. But authority basically lies with the three Orders, and the sacramental powers of the priesthood cannot be shared with those who are not ordained priest.

A note on priestly celibacy

In the Eastern Orthodox and Eastern Catholic Churches priests – but not bishops – may be married. In the Latin Rite, a few married non-Catholic ministers who have become Catholics have been ordained as priests. But normally Latin Rite priests must be *celibate*, unmarried. The purpose of this rule is partly practical. For example, it leaves priests free of family commitments so that they have more time to serve their parishes and may care for their people with less danger of jealousy arising. The rule could be changed if the practical benefits of allowing priests to be married seemed to warrant it. Celibacy is not a constitutive part of the priesthood, whereas it is for the consecration of religious.

It may be that a desire to keep a significant distance between sexual intercourse and the celebration of the Eucharist lay behind the repeated attempts of the West to enforce celibacy, and behind the rule still current in the East that priests should abstain from sexual relations with their wives before celebrating the Holy Eucharist (not celebrated daily by all Eastern priests). We should not suppose that this implies that sex is 'unholy'; after all, the Old Testament both celebrates sex and keeps it away from the Temple. Rather, we should note that sexual intercourse is a good that speaks of God's blessing on *this* life, in which the human race must be propagated, and will have no place in the immortal life of the resurrection world, in which 'they neither marry nor are given in marriage'. On the other hand, the Eucharist is a pledge of the heavenly banquet, the marriage feast of the Lamb, and is food for our journey to that goal. In a society more attuned to symbolism than our own, the need for those who offer the Eucharist to turn from what stands for our present life to what stands for the future Kingdom may have been a symbol of the hope that should drive us all.

A note on the question of women's ordination

The Catholic and the Orthodox Churches consider that women cannot be ordained, and this has sometimes been defended on the grounds that they are not fit to govern. It would be hard to maintain that proposition nowadays! But we may note that in all the sacraments there has to be an element of historical continuity with what Christ did in Palestine 2,000 years ago. We may celebrate Mass in English rather than Aramaic or Hebrew, but we must always use wheat bread and grape wine, for that is what Christ used. They were the appropriate material for that and for many other cultures. There are cultures in which they would not be the obvious food and drink, but wheat bread and grape wine must still be used there – imported if necessary – because it is more important to do what Christ did, in union with the whole Church, than to compose a local rite that does not so well point back to the historical Jesus. Maybe, because Christ chose only men to be leaders in His Church, we must continue to use the same 'material' for the sake of doing what He did. In His own society, and in many others, women were not 'leadership material' – perhaps for invalid reasons, such as a supposed psychological weakness, perhaps for practical reasons, such as being too often engaged in child-bearing. In our culture, women have 'leadership potential', and their skills and talents should be used in the Church as fully as possible; but when it comes to the sacrament of Orders, we must do what Christ did, in union with the Church of other times and places.

MARRIAGE: COVENANT IN CHRIST

The marriage covenant, by which a man and a woman set up between themselves a community involving the whole of life, ordered by its nature to the good of the spouses and to the procreation and education of offspring, was raised among the baptized to the dignity of a sacrament by Christ the Lord.

(Code of Canon Law, canon 1055)

By coming to restore the original order of creation disturbed by sin, [Jesus] himself gives the strength and grace to live marriage in the new dimension of the Reign of God . . . It can seem difficult, even impossible, to bind oneself for life to another human being. This makes it all the more important to proclaim the Good News that God loves us with a definitive and irrevocable love, that married couples share in this love, that it supports and sustains them, and that by their own faithfulness they can be witnesses to God's faithful love.

(*Catechism* 1615, 1648)

The other sacraments are specifically Christian rituals, though parallel rituals are found in many societies and religions. In the sacrament of *Marriage*, a ritual which is important in every society itself becomes a Christian ritual, a revelation of Christ's love, a means of grace.

At the beginning of the Bible, the marriage of Adam and Eve is portrayed, and it is said that a man becomes one flesh with his wife. The institution of marriage is found in every society, though in very varied forms, some of which might be judged as more or less dehumanizing, especially to women. As a human reality, it is meant to be a source of great fulfilment for the individuals concerned and for society. It provides mutual support, it calls upon love, loyalty, care and respect between husband and wife, it provides a stable context for the joy and self-giving of sexual intercourse with the emotions this arouses, it serves to propagate the human race, and it provides a home in which children can be cared for and brought up. Although in some societies polygamy and divorce have been acceptable, Jewish tradition before Christ shows an increasing preference for monogamy, and divorce is attacked by the (late) prophet Malachi (2:16). This suggests that even at the natural level, monogamy and life-long fidelity are the ideal, and lead most readily to human fulfilment. In support of this, the relationship between God and His people is presented in the Old Testament as a marriage bond between one husband and one wife, which the divine husband does not allow the wife's infidelities to sever.

Jesus taught that divorce was contrary to God's original plan, and had been allowed because of people's 'hardness of heart' (Mark 10:2–12). For His disciples, therefore, the original plan is to be followed: He gives those who marry in Him the strength they need to live their marriages with life-long fidelity. This is one reason for seeing Christian Marriage as a sacrament: Christ is at work in it, providing healing grace and promoting faithful love, making it possible to resist temptations to unfaithfulness.

A sacrament must symbolize the saving work of Christ. The covenant, the promise of life-long loyalty, between the bride and groom is a symbol of the New Covenant made on the cross, when Christ gave Himself for the life of His bride, the Church. A sacrament has an 'objective' element that does not depend on the holiness of those involved. In the Eucharist this is Christ's presence, in Baptism it is character, in Marriage it is the marriage-bond established by the vows, the consecration of husband and wife to each other. There is also an element which can be thwarted if those who receive the sacrament are not open to grace: husband and wife have access to Christ's help, so that serving Him in each other they may grow as Christians. If they make use of this help, their unity in one flesh and in faithful love is an on-going symbol of the continuing faithfulness between Christ and His body, the Church. The fruitfulness of their marriage, in terms of mutual fulfilment, offspring, the growth of the family and the peace of society, is a symbol of the fruitful care of Christ for His Church, and her response to His grace. A sacrament must also look forward to the Kingdom, and the joy and communion of Marriage point us forward to the joy and communion of Heaven, 'the marriage-feast of the Lamb'.

Because marriage is not a private affair, but part of the structure of the societies to which the couple belong, Catholics must marry in accordance with the law of the Church, which normally means they must make their marriage vows before a priest and two other witnesses.[5] Eastern Christians, whether Catholic or Orthodox, must also follow the law of their Church. Otherwise, marriages may be validly made according to civil law and custom; and non-Catholic Christians who marry confer the sacrament on each other as do a Catholic bride and groom. They are ministers of Christ, bringing each other the power of the love He showed in His self-giving.

On occasion, a marriage which is not a sacrament, because not made in Christ, or one which is not consummated so that the couple have not become one flesh, may be broken off by divorce; but the state should legislate carefully in this area, recognizing that an atmosphere which trivializes commitments such as marriage vows is damaging, and taking care that children do not suffer from broken homes. A marriage which is sacramental and consummated cannot be dissolved by any human power. An *annulment* granted by a Catholic marriage tribunal is not a divorce, but a recognition that there was never a real marriage – perhaps the couple could not, or clearly did not, make a commitment to each other that could count as a marriage vow. If someone is abandoned by his or her spouse, or if, as a result of great difficulties, a couple agree to separate, remarriage is not possible if the original marriage was validly made in Christ, and consummated. An abandoned spouse is called to reflect God's behaviour towards His people when they were unfaithful, and not react with infidelity. A civil divorce (even if justified as a practical arrangement) does not destroy the sacramental bond.

Many happily married couples have weathered difficulties together, and their relationship is all the more precious for having been worked at. They bear witness to values such as loyalty and perseverance, and give encouragement to new couples contemplating marriage. Christ's help must be sought all the more urgently nowadays, when trial relationships are seen by many as acceptable, and there is less support from the 'extended family', from friends and from neighbours than perhaps there used to be.

There is much more to married love than sex, and sometimes, perhaps out of respect for the other partner, it is right to abstain from sex for a while. But sexual intercourse finds its place in marriage – and nowhere else – since it is a mutual self-giving that expresses and cements the couple's pledge of loyalty to each other. Outside the context of marriage it involves some contradiction. For example, in committing adultery a man says to his mistress 'I give myself to you totally and not totally'. In intercourse he gives himself totally; by being pledged to his wife he cannot give himself to his mistress. And worse, he contradicts his covenant with his wife: having pledged exclusive loyalty to her, he now gives himself to another. An element of the whole meaning of sexual intercourse is also contradicted if a barrier is placed in the way of its openness to offspring. Part of the dignity of sexual intercourse is its role in procreation, for, as we saw in Chapter 1, the Creator is specially involved in the conception of a human being, and parents are called to share in a noble way in God's life-giving work.

NOTES

1 See *Summa*, III, 61, 3 ad 2. We do not need to judge what truth and what falsehood there are in the rites of non-Christians, since when we bring the Gospel to them, they are called to move from the obscure to the clear, just as the Jewish Law, once a thing of glory, had to yield to the greater glory of Christ (2 Corinthians 3:10). Elements of local culture should be used in Christian liturgy in missionary areas as far as possible, just as its Jewish roots must be preserved in the liturgy generally; and missionaries should be sensitive to the insights their audience already possess at the same time as they seek to show them that their deepest longings find their home in Christ.

2 This would explain why, according to the Acts of the Apostles, the first Christians were baptized 'in the name of Jesus'. Being Jews, they already believed in God the Father; and it was clear from the gifts He gave that the Spirit was at work among Jesus' followers. Those converts only needed to proclaim their faith in Jesus. Faith in the three divine Persons had to be proclaimed once the Church began to expand beyond the confines of Judaism.

3 Children in danger of death were still baptized, as nearly happened with St Augustine, and he makes theological use of the custom of baptizing children 'for the forgiveness of sins'.

4 The 'Limbo of the unbaptized' is not the same as the 'Limbo of the Fathers' from which the soul of the dead Christ released those who had died hoping for Him.

5 For a good reason, the local bishop may allow a Catholic and a non-Catholic Christian to marry before a non-Catholic minister. He may also allow a Catholic to marry a non-Christian – in this case, the marriage is a valuable human reality, but not a sacrament, though it is still celebrated before a priest and receives his blessing.

CHAPTER 10

REPENTANCE AND HEALING

THE SACRAMENT OF RECONCILIATION

Christ instituted the sacrament of Penance for all sinful members of his Church: above all for those who, since Baptism, have fallen into grave sin, and have thus lost their baptismal grace and wounded ecclesial communion. It is to them that the sacrament of Penance offers a new possibility to convert and to recover the grace of justification . . . [The] fundamental structure [of this sacrament] comprises two equally essential elements: on the one hand, the acts of the man who undergoes conversion through the action of the Holy Spirit: namely, contrition, confession and satisfaction; on the other, God's action through the intervention of the Church . . . In this sacrament, the sinner, placing himself before the merciful judgement of God, *anticipates* in a certain way *the judgement* to which he will be subjected at the end of his earthly life . . .

(Catechism 1446, 1448, 1470)

'CHRIST Jesus came into the world to save sinners' (1 Timothy 1:15). Because of the Fall we are all born in need of saving and forgiving. The power to save is in Christ's Passion and Resurrection, for He opened His arms on the cross to draw into one those who were alienated from God, from each other, and from themselves, and He rose from the dead to be our source of new life. This saving power is brought to bear on us in Baptism, in which all our sins are forgiven. Forgiveness, we have seen, is the work of God's love in which He makes those who have been sinners into His friends. So the forgiveness of sins and the coming of the divine life are two aspects of one new birth, rather as Christ's death and Resurrection are two phases of the Paschal Mystery we are called to enter into.

177

Our unity with God and each other is nourished by the Holy Eucharist, and the key ministries in which our life as His people is manifest are established by the sacraments of Confirmation, Orders and Marriage. But we also need a sacrament that can restore unity with God and the Church when it is lost, a sacrament in which we are brought back to life in God after mortal sin. For we are able to turn from God after Baptism and cease to be His friends, and then we need once more to be saved from our sins, we need to receive afresh the forgiveness Christ won for us on the cross.

The sacrament for the forgiveness of sins committed after Baptism is sometimes called *Confession*, after one of its components. Because it reconciles us with God and with the Church from whose fellowship we have turned, it is often called the sacrament of *Reconciliation*. In Latin it is called *sacramentum Paenitentiae*, which is normally translated as 'sacrament of Penance' – in fact, another component of the rite is to 'do penance'. But a better translation might be *sacrament of Repentance*, for it is the ritual by which we repent of our sins, turning back to the God whose love draws us and makes us alive again.

A human relationship may be broken by some offence, and can be mended when the one who did the wrong acknowledges his fault and is sorry. He must wish he had not committed the offence, and be determined not to repeat it; he must apologize to the one he has wronged, seeking forgiveness, and this may well involve a gesture of amendment or sorrow. It is the same with God. If we break off our relationship with Him, we must acknowledge our fault, *confessing* it to the minister who represents Him. We must be *contrite*, sorry for our sins, because they are a disloyalty to the Friend who is so good and whose love we have rejected. Our sorrow must involve a wish that we had not committed sin and a *purpose of amendment*, the intention not to repeat the sin. We must perform some *penance*, a gesture of sorrow which also begins the work of *satisfaction*, that is the making-good, the restoring of the wholeness that is virtue when sin has led to the warping that is vice. When a human relationship is repaired, a word or gesture of forgiveness is needed from the one who has been wronged, and again it is the same with God. The minister to whom we confess our sins and who sets the penance, also speaks words of forgiveness on God's behalf. The central words are: 'I absolve you from your sins.' The words are words of *absolution*, that is, of setting free, because repentance is God's work. He is active in the whole process just described, bringing us back to Himself, saving us from our sins. When we have wronged human beings we seek their forgiveness; when we have wronged God He seeks out and brings back the lost. His work is carried out and shown us in the sacrament.

The sacrament of Repentance looks back to Christ's ministry, in which He preached repentance and spoke words of reconciliation, such as: 'Neither do I condemn you; go, and do not sin again' (John 8:11). It looks back to His crucifixion, at which He prayed for our forgiveness, and which can draw us to respond to God's love. Any anguish we feel over our sins, whatever prayers we say or whatever acts of self-denial we perform as our penance, are a small sharing in the anguish, prayer and self-giving of Christ. The sacrament looks back to Christ's Resurrection which brought us new life, after which He appeared to the disciples and gave them authority in the Holy Spirit to forgive sins.[1] In the sacrament we share in Christ's journey to new life, and the Spirit of love unites us again to the Father as His children.

The sacrament of Repentance also looks forward to the final judgement, when all our sins will be revealed – but, we hope, revealed as forgiven, so that they will be a cause of thanksgiving and not sadness. A priest may never disclose sins told him in Confession, nor make use of knowledge gained in Confession. The secret confession of sins both reveals and veils the public scrutiny of God, as all the sacraments show us His Kingdom yet veil its glory. The joy of reconciliation is an anticipation of the communion of the Kingdom in which all evil and division will have been overcome.

Mortal sin impedes the exercise of our baptismal priesthood, for while we do not want to be built up in love we cannot share fully in the Holy Eucharist with all God's people, by receiving Holy Communion. So the sacrament of Repentance restores us to our vigour as members of the Church, and the priest who speaks God's words of absolution is also the Church's representative, reconciling us with her. Therefore he must have authority from the Church to absolve; ordination by itself is not enough. We should not suppose that going to the Church's minister for forgiveness somehow puts a man between us and God; as in all the sacraments the rite is God Himself reaching out to us through His ministers in the richest possible way, a way which suits our needs and builds up our community in Christ. Therefore the Church asks us to go to Confession at least once a year, and to confess all our mortal sins, not because she wants to control God's forgiveness, but because we must not despise the means of liberation He has offered.[2]

While it is necessary for the undoing of mortal sin, Confession is also important for venial sin. In the early Church this sacrament was only offered for very serious sins (and only offered once), and it involved public penance such as long fasts. The Celtic monks began to employ confession and set penances for lesser sins, and this practice spread throughout the Church. Since venial sins do not destroy our share in God's life, they are forgiven or overcome by whatever promotes an increase in charity and therefore in integrity. The Holy Eucharist does this with special power. Other rites, like blessings, prayers and gestures of sorrow, acts of self-denial and of charity, and so on, all remit venial sin. In Confession, however, we have a sacrament specially designed for the forgiveness of sin, which promotes honesty and humility, and which provides an opportunity for advice and encouragement.

The penances we are asked to perform are nowadays token in nature, gestures of repentance that do not pretend to complete the work of reorientating our affections and uprooting vices. Therefore the liberation from sin that was complete in Baptism is not normally complete in the sacrament of Penance. Once we have returned to sin after Baptism, its undoing requires a more conscious sharing in Christ's liberating Passion. Therefore the Church encourages us to perform works of self-denial in addition to the penances set in Confession, especially during Lent, when we commemorate Christ's fast at the beginning of His ministry and His Passion at its end. We are asked to do penance on Fridays; in Great Britain Catholics may abstain from meat (a luxury for many people for much of history) or perform some other work of prayer, self-denial or charity. On Ash Wednesday and Good Friday those over 14 should abstain from meat, and adults (other than the elderly, the sick and those engaged in heavy work) are to fast by only taking one full meal and two snacks.[3]

The undoing of vice is completed in Purgatory. The Church helps the living and the dead in the work of undoing sin in all sorts of ways, and most of all by the Eucharistic Sacrifice, which obtains the forgiveness of sins for the living and the dead. She offers us *indulgences*; that is, certain acts of devotion and charity are enriched by the Church's gift so that their effectiveness is increased. Since she is the body of Christ, the liberating grace of Christ is at work in her, and the prayers and efforts of each member – especially those who are closest to God – help all. The work of love Christ carried out in His own person and still carries out in His members constitutes a kind of 'treasury', which the Church dispenses by granting indulgences so that our journey to God through Purgatory will be speeded or we may even fly straight to Him. We may 'transfer' indulgences we have gained to the souls already in Purgatory, that their journey may be speeded.

THE ANOINTING OF THE SICK

[Jesus] makes [his disciples] share in his ministry of compassion and healing . . . The risen Lord renews this mission . . . and confirms it through the signs that the Church performs by invoking his name. These signs demonstrate in a special way that Jesus is truly 'God who saves' . . . the apostolic Church has its own rite for the sick, attested to by St James . . . The first grace of this sacrament is one of strengthening, peace and courage to overcome the difficulties that go with the condition of serious illness or the frailty of old age . . . This assistance from the Lord by the power of his Spirit is meant to lead the sick person to healing of the soul, but also of the body if such is God's will . . . This last anointing fortifies the end of our earthly life like a solid rampart for the final struggle before entering the Father's house.

(*Catechism* 1506–1507, 1510, 1520, 1523)

Jesus healed the sick, and sent His Apostles out to do the same. St Mark tells us (6:13) that they anointed with oil many that were sick and healed them. In the Letter of St James (5:14) we are told that the elders of the Church should pray over sick people and anoint them with oil in the name of the Lord. This practice has been carried out in the Church ever since. The oil to be used is now normally blessed on Maundy Thursday by the bishop, who invokes the Holy Spirit upon it. Those who are seriously ill, or are nearing death through old age, may be anointed by a priest. After laying his hands on them, he anoints at least their foreheads and hands, saying: 'Through this holy anointing may the Lord in His love and mercy help you with the grace of the Holy Spirit. May the Lord who frees you from sin save you and raise you up.'

The Anointing of the Sick is for the sick; Holy Communion – Viaticum, food for the journey – is the sacrament of the dying. Sickness and the weakness of old age do not cut us off from God – on the contrary, we can make use of them as a means of identifying ourselves with Christ in His suffering – but they can make it difficult to take part in the public worship and witness of the Church with full vigour. Therefore the sick should be anointed at the *beginning* of their illness, and whenever it moves to a new stage, in the hope of their being restored to the Church.[4] But quite obviously not all the sick who are anointed do recover, and eventually everyone dies, if not always of sickness or old age. Does this imply that the sacrament does not always work? Since in it Jesus reaches out to touch the sick, how can it fail to work? The sacrament does have a healing power, but, like all the sacraments, it is a sacrament of hope. It points us forward to God's Kingdom, giving us power to be part of that Kingdom, and presents us with that Kingdom through its symbolism and through the growth within us of the life that will flourish there. So when the sacrament does lead to healing, this is a sign of the resurrection world beyond sickness and death, and the Spirit is given so that the person who has been healed can make good use of renewed vigour as a member of God's pilgrim people. And when physical healing does not result, the sacrament still does bring the strength and help of the Holy Spirit, so that the sick or elderly person may more closely identify with Christ in His suffering and dying and journey to new life. Thus the sick person is made able to go forward more securely into the resurrection world, and in the end the sacrament does bring healing.

The Anointing of the Sick looks back to the healing work of Christ. His miracles of healing were a sign of the 'breaking-in' of the new age that had been prophesied. When He shone with glory at His Transfiguration the Apostles had a glimpse of the glory we are to share. He taught His followers that they would have to follow Him on the way of the cross if they were to share His glory. And in His Resurrection He went ahead of us into bliss as our Pioneer. The oil that glistens on the body of the sick person symbolizes not only the glory of Christ glimpsed 2,000 years ago, but also the 'robe of glory' we hope to wear once sickness, death and sin have been finally defeated and we can be with Christ in the Kingdom, with the Christ who is with us in the sacraments to help us on our way.

NOTES

1 John 20:23 reads: 'If you forgive the sins of any, they are forgiven; if you retain the sins of any, they are retained.' The Church is charged to minister forgiveness generously, but she may sometimes have to speak with something of the sharpness with which Christ challenged sinners. We can make dishonest gestures of feigned sorrow towards human beings and towards God, and since His minister may occasionally need to say 'You still need to become sorry for your sin', Jesus speaks of the possibility of 'retaining sin'.

2 Just as the desire for Baptism can lay hold on a share in the life Baptism gives, so the life of grace can be restored before we confess our sins. The God who leads people to faith and draws them to seek Baptism also leads people to repent and draws them to confess their sins. So if you have committed a mortal sin, and have become repentant, you have already received forgiveness – but it would be difficult to claim that you had become repentant if you despised the sign of Reconciliation offered and refused to perform the gesture of sorrow asked.

3 This form of fasting and abstinence is not very demanding! It is a gesture that most of us can perform together, and so it can lead to humility – we recognize that we are all mediocre sinners and mediocre saints, all needing healing for unexciting sins. More demanding penances, if wisely chosen, can do more to cure vice, but also bring with them the danger of pride, for we can be tempted to boast of what we achieve.

4 The sacrament of the Sick used to be called *Extrema Unctio*, rendered into English as 'Extreme Unction'. This gave the impression it was for those '*in extremis*', whereas in fact the Latin simply means 'last anointing'. Christians receive a series of anointings: at Baptism, in Confirmation, and (for some) at Ordination. The Anointing of the Sick is the last in the series.

CHAPTER 11

THE CHURCH, THE BODY OF CHRIST

THE COMMUNITY OF JESUS' DISCIPLES

'The Church' is the People that God gathers in the whole world. She exists in local communities and is made real as a liturgical, above all a Eucharistic, assembly. She draws her life from the word and the Body of Christ and so herself becomes Christ's Body . . . [The Church] is catholic because Christ is present in her . . . In her subsists the fullness of Christ's Body united with its Head; this implies that she receives from him 'the fullness of the means of salvation' which he has willed: correct and complete confession of faith, full sacramental life, and ordained ministry in apostolic succession . . . [The Church] is catholic because she has been sent out by Christ on a mission to the whole of the human race . . . the Eucharist makes the Church. Those who receive the Eucharist are united more closely to Christ. Through it Christ unites them to all the faithful in one body – the Church.

(Catechism 752, 830–831, 1396)

ONE of the most influential books of all time is St Augustine's *City of God*. He looks back to the biblical story of Cain and Abel, the first two children of Adam and Eve, in which Cain and his descendants build a worldly city of violence, and Abel, God's friend, is the first victim of violence, killed before he can have physical descendants. Augustine pictures two cities growing from that beginning of human history: the city of this world, opposed to God, destined to perish, and the City of God, built up of His friends, living by His values, and looking forward to eternal bliss in the next world. In this way Augustine presented to his contemporaries and to subsequent centuries the biblical story of salvation, in which God breaks

184

into this fallen world, calling people to be His friends and leading them by the pilgrimage of faith to the heavenly city lit up by His glory. In our own time the Second Vatican Council has put forward afresh the vision of God's pilgrim People, called to live in this world and show it God's care and loving call, while going forward in hope to His Kingdom.

The Greek word we translate as *church* is *ekklēsia*, which comes from the verb meaning 'to call out'. So, most basically, the Church is the assembly of all those whom God has called out of the fallen world to be His friends, and who have not definitively abandoned their place in His people.[1] Following St Augustine, St Thomas saw the Church as existing from the beginning of the human race. But, because it is only in Christ that we can be saved, he claimed that all who become God's friends and share His life do so on the basis of faith in Christ. The faith of those who lived before Christ was implicit, a response to promises in which God spoke more or less clearly of the Saviour He would send. The faith of those who live after Christ is to be more explicit. We have seen ways in which the saving work of Christ was presented to the Jewish people, and to those who did not have the benefit of the Jewish Law; and we have seen how Christ's work is presented to us in the Scriptures and the Christian sacraments. There may be people today to whom Christ is still shown through the Jewish Law and even through other rites and traditions, but we must preach to the world the full revelation of God's love shown us in Christ and in what He did and suffered, so that people may respond with greater gratitude.

Since those who are brought to an explicit faith in Christ are clearly and visibly called by God to be His friends, the word 'Church' can refer more narrowly to the *Christian Church*. This began with the *company of disciples* Jesus gathered round Himself; it was prefigured in the history of Israel, has spread in the power of the Holy Spirit, and is found throughout the world. Jesus gave a special role to the twelve Apostles within the company of His disciples, and within the body of the Twelve He gave a special role to Peter. Jesus' teachings and the power of His Paschal Mystery were to be kept alive among His disciples by the work of the Spirit He sent them. If you look for a body of disciples that has grown without a break from the group that followed Jesus in Palestine, and which has preserved all that He gave them, you find the *Roman Catholic Church*. In her, the role of the Apostles is perpetuated by the bishops, and that of Peter by the Bishop of Rome. In the power of the Holy Spirit and in fidelity to the Scriptures she expounds with authority the teachings of Jesus, and celebrates His sacraments. Therefore the Roman Catholic Church can claim to be the Christian Church in an unqualified sense, while recognizing that there are truly Christian Churches and communities not visibly united with her.

The title, *Catholic* (universal), expresses the Church's claim to preserve all that Jesus gave His followers, and her world-wide mission. As the Church spread over the centuries and took root in different cultures, various 'groupings' of dioceses emerged. These all preserved the same faith and the same sacraments, but evolved their own liturgical, spiritual and theological traditions, and their own laws and customs. So there are today many *Catholic Churches of the Eastern Rite*, acknowledging the authority of the Pope but preserving traditions that grew up in areas of Eastern Europe, the Mediterranean world and the Middle East. They contribute in an important way to the catholicity of the Church. In Western Europe (and, until the spread of Islam, in North Africa), Latin came to be used as the main language of liturgy and theology. Because of the way the Church expanded outside Europe from the sixteenth century, the *Latin* or *Western Rite* is now by far the largest grouping within the Catholic Church. Within it, too, there have been and are different liturgical customs, spiritual traditions and theological schools. The Church preserves a balance of unity and diversity.

The unity of God's people has been sadly damaged over the centuries, beginning with the separation of the Christian Church and the Jewish Synagogue. Divisions arose because of the Catholic Church's leniency towards sinners and because of disagreements over the Trinity and the Incarnation, aggravated by political factors and failures in mutual understanding. The *Eastern Orthodox Churches*, of which the largest are the Greek and Russian Orthodox Churches, deserve special mention, for they can trace their history back to the Apostles, and have preserved all that Christ left His Church, except communion with the successor of Peter. The Catholic Church recognizes their sacraments and their laws; there are disagreements (which need to be taken seriously) over the relationship between the

Holy Spirit and the Son, the precise authority of the Pope, and the legitimacy of divorce. The Churches and Christian communities deriving from the Protestant Reformation read the Scriptures with devotion and cherish many important Christian doctrines. Their Baptism is valid, and their members who marry do so in Christ, so that their marriages are sacramental. In many cases, at least, these Churches and communities rejected the Catholic structure of Orders or the Catholic understanding of the priesthood, so that their ordination rites could no longer signify, and therefore could not effect, a valid priesthood. Nevertheless, their ministers still perform a valuable role, and the worship they lead helps many people grow as Jesus' disciples.

We must have a concern for *ecumenism*, the attempt to re-establish unity among Christians. Jesus prayed that His followers might be one, and a united witness to the Gospel would be more effective. We should pray for unity; and it is good to meet with our fellow Christians, to discuss our faith together, to pray with each other in appropriate ways, and to co-operate in forms of witness and in charitable works.

Rather as God's life in us is naturally expressed in works of charity, so the Church as a supernatural reality is properly expressed in the form of a visible, structured body. Her nature has been expressed by means of a variety of images. She can be seen as the Bride of Christ, born from His pierced side as He slept on the cross, as (in the story) Eve was taken from Adam's side as he slept. Christ gave Himself for her life, and the mutual self-giving of bride and groom in Marriage is a sacrament of Christ's cherishing of the Church and her fidelity to Him. The marriage between Christ and the Church is fruitful: not only does she bring forth good works, she also brings new members of Christ to birth in Baptism. So she is also Mother, Mother of Christians and, in a sense, Mother of Christ as well as His Bride.

One specially helpful image for the Church is *the Mystical Body of Christ*. Jesus spoke of Himself as the vine of which we are the branches, and St Paul spoke of Christ living in us and of us being members of His body, partly as his way of showing that we draw life from Christ, and partly to encourage us to care for each other and respect each other's gifts. The fact that the Church is Christ's body makes it possible to see our prayer, our work and our suffering as a share in Christ's prayer, work and suffering – or, rather, He prays, works and suffers in us. The many ways in which the actions of the Church mediate between us and God are not ways in which men get between us and God, but ways in which God reaches out to us wisely and helpfully. He reaches out through His Son, the unique Mediator, and from thence through His Son's members and ministers, so that human relationships, spoiled by sin, are healed by becoming channels of grace. The body of Christ which we are, is built up by Christ's actions. His reconciling power reaches out, especially through the sacraments, and most of all through the Eucharist, which symbolizes and brings about the body of Christ – both His human body, and, through that body, His mystical body. Because the ministers of the sacraments are His members, we can say that the sacraments are actions of the Church, Christ being at work in her. The Holy Spirit who formed the human body of Jesus and was at work in His ministry, is given by Him to the Church, especially through the sacraments, to form and enliven His mystical body and to direct the ministry of His members. *The Spirit is the Soul of the Church.*

A note on intercommunion

Since the Eucharist makes the Church, it might seem that the unity of Christians would be promoted by us all celebrating the Eucharist together, but this is not appropriate. When a Catholic marries a non-Catholic Christian in accordance with the Church's law, the sacrament of Marriage is of course celebrated. For a grave and pressing need a Catholic may ask a priest of a Church whose Orders we recognize for Communion, Confession or Anointing; and for a similar need, and under certain conditions, non-Catholics may receive those sacraments from a Catholic priest. Otherwise a contradiction is involved in 'inter-communion'. For the Eucharist is meant to build up the unity of the Church, and this is a unity of faith, in which we are 'of one mind' (Philippians 2:2), and a unity of practical charity, in which we live as one community under the same leaders. To receive Communion together speaks of the desire for this unity; but if those who receive mean to go away from the altar as members of different bodies, living under different leaders and not sharing a common mind, there is a lack of fit between their public expression of unity (however well meant) and their public belonging to separated communities.

AUTHORITY, TEACHING AND WITNESS

> The Lord Jesus endowed his community with a structure that will remain until the Kingdom is fully achieved. Before all else there is the choice of the Twelve with Peter as their head . . . This pastoral office of Peter and the other apostles belongs to the Church's very foundation and is continued by the bishops under the primacy of the Pope . . . In order to preserve the Church in the purity of the faith handed on by the apostles, Christ who is the Truth willed to confer on her a share in his own infallibility . . . In the Church, which is like [a] sacrament . . . the consecrated life is seen as a special sign of the mystery of Redemption.
>
> (*Catechism* 765, 881, 889, 932)

> The pilgrim Church is missionary by her very nature.
> (Vatican II, *Decree on the Missionary Activity of the Church*, 2)

Jesus chose twelve Apostles. This action, and imagery found in St Paul and the Apocalypse, attribute a 'foundational role' to them. So we claim that the bishops, their successors, to whom they handed on authority, are charged to preserve the faith and unity of the body of disciples. We saw something of the bishops' role in Chapter 9. One of the twelve, Simon Peter, was given his second name – 'Rock' – by Jesus, and charged to strengthen his brethren and to feed Jesus' sheep (see Matthew 16:18; Luke 22:32; John 1:42 and 21:15ff.). Peter's role in the Church is fulfilled by the Pope, focus of the Church's unity. He has the highest authority among those who govern the Church on earth, and by being in communion with Rome each local Church, governed by its bishop, is held within the body of disciples to which Simon Peter once ministered on earth.

The Church has, on the surface, developed greatly since her first years. Someone observing a Papal ceremony in the Baroque era, and the prayer-meeting of a small fundamentalist sect, might suppose that the latter was closer to the first Christian meetings described in the Acts of the Apostles. But someone comparing an acorn, a hazelnut and an oak tree might suppose that the closest similarity was between the first two, whereas in fact the acorn grows into the oak tree – they are the same thing. The Roman Catholic Church of today, and the original body of disciples, are the same thing. That is true also of the Church's doctrine: the faith of the Church today, and the faith of the first disciples, are identical. It is said, and said truly, that the Church's doctrine develops. From the original 'deposit of faith' the Church has drawn out and made explicit what was implicit – but she has not invented new truths, she has preserved what was left her by Jesus. Cardinal Newman wrote a famous *Essay on the Development of Christian Doctrine*, proposing tests for 'authentic developments' – which amount to ways of showing that beneath the obvious developments there is continuity, the kind of continuity found in a growing organism.

Because she is 'incarnate' in history, the Church possesses *tradition*: within the varied, developing body of liturgical and theological traditions there is *handed on* the Church's faith and identity. Within the life of God's people, the Scriptures have been composed and preserved, the sacraments instituted and celebrated; and one generation has taught the next the wonder of God's ways and how to serve Him. All this can be seen as an exercise of tradition. Alternatively, we can see tradition as the other ways beside Scripture in which truth has been handed down from the Apostles. There is no disagreement between Scripture, tradition and authority in the Church; and it may be that there is nothing in tradition that is not at least hinted at in Scripture.

As the body of Christ, enlivened by the Spirit of truth, the Church is *infallible*. That is, she preserves the truth revealed in Christ, and cannot commit herself to error as she unfolds and proclaims it. Those who hold authority in the Church and are charged to watch over her unity and fidelity can declare in the name of the Church what it is she believes, and in so doing they exercise her infallibility. We have seen occasions when the doctrines of the Trinity and the Incarnation were debated, and Ecumenical Councils, and the Tome of Leo, set out the true faith authentically and rejected erroneous accounts of the faith. Ecumenical Councils, and the Pope as supreme Pastor, may declare infallibly what the Church's faith is; and we may also gather what it is she believes by examining oft-repeated or universally agreed teachings of the Pope and body of bishops as they exercise their pastoral role of building up the disciples' understanding of their faith. The liturgy of the Church, the devotion of the faithful, and the consensus of theologians, are also witnesses to the belief of the Church.

Not only the bishops, but all the faithful, are called to bear witness to Christ. The Church is by her nature a missionary Church. St Peter tells us to 'be prepared to make a defence to any one who calls you to account for the hope that is in you' (1 Peter 3:15). Some members of the Church are called to be missionaries in a dramatic way, leaving their homes to spread the Gospel elsewhere; some are called to be teachers of the faith in universities, schools, parishes and so on. Some people are called to bear witness to God's Kingdom by joining *religious orders*, or by other forms of *consecrated life*. They dedicate themselves by means of vows to a certain way of life, typically involving *obedience, celibacy and poverty*. The ways in which such vows operate vary from one institute to another: obedience may take the form of 'availability for mission', and poverty often means 'community of goods'. Some orders are dedicated to prayer and contemplation, some to more active forms of service. Marriage has the dignity of a sacrament: it reveals in its depths the power of Christ's love. But it may be seen by those without the faith as merely a human institution. By contrast, the consecration of religious to their way of life is not a sacrament, but can strike many people as something odd that does not make sense except in the light of Christian hope. So it is a form of life that bears witness to Christ, who was unmarried and consecrated to His ministry; and it gives voice to our hope for the Kingdom.

MARY, THE MODEL DISCIPLE, AND THE COMMUNION OF SAINTS

By celebrating the passage of [the] saints from earth to heaven, the Church proclaims the paschal mystery as achieved in the saints who have suffered and been glorified with Christ; she proposes them to the faithful as examples who draw all to the Father through Christ, and through their merits she pleads for God's favours . . . Redeemed in an especially sublime manner by reason of the merits of her Son . . . [Mary] is endowed with the supreme office and dignity of being the Mother of the Son of

God . . . she is . . . the mother of the members of Christ . . . the
Church's model and excellent exemplar in faith and charity . . .
In the bodily and spiritual glory which she possesses in heaven,
the Mother of Jesus continues in this present world as the image
and first flowering of the Church as she is to be perfected in the
world to come.

> (Vatican II, *Constitution on the Sacred Liturgy*, 104;
> *Dogmatic Constitution on the Church*, 53 and 68)

The Church is not merely an earthly reality. Those who have
died in Christ are still His members, and we are still in
communion with them. Those who are in Purgatory can be
helped by our prayers; those who enjoy the vision of God can
help us by their prayers. The charity that moves us to pray for
each other and support each other in our pilgrimage is not
brought to an end by death.

Our perseverance on our journey is assisted by the witness of
others to the power of God's love as well as by their prayers, and
just as the Bible holds up for our encouragement a 'great cloud
of witnesses' (Hebrews 12:1), so also the Church puts forward
many *saints* whose holiness has been publicly recognized. Their
memory is celebrated in the liturgy at the international or local
level. Many friends of God have touched other people's lives
with His love in quiet ways that have not come to public notice,
so that their high position in Heaven is not yet known. On 1
November each year, All Saints' Day, the Church celebrates all
her unknown brothers and sisters in Heaven, and on the
following day, All Souls' Day, she prays with special intensity
for all those who are in Purgatory and still on their way to glory.

Besides talking to God in prayer, we quite naturally talk to
each other, and all our conversation may be deepened by
charity. Sometimes as we talk to others we ask them to pray for
us, and in this way we bear witness to the value of prayer and
our solidarity in Christ. It is not at all odd, then, but valuable,
to talk to the saints and to ask them for their prayers. Indeed,
part of the process by which the Church comes to recognize
someone as a saint is the discovery that his or her prayers are
powerful and can obtain a miracle from God.

The greatest of all saints (except, of course, Christ in His
humanity, the source of all holiness) is the *Virgin Mary*, Mother
of Christ and therefore *Mother of God*. She may be seen as the

model disciple, from whom we can learn about the following of Christ. She was naturally involved in the birth and infancy of Christ, and we are told that she treasured up and pondered in her heart the events that occurred, as we must do in our contemplation. She accepted the Father's will that she should be the Mother of the Messiah: 'I am the handmaid of the Lord; let it be to me according to your word' (Luke 1:38). If we can imitate her obedience, Christ who was conceived in her will also dwell in us. Bearing Christ in her womb Mary went to visit her cousin Elizabeth, who was expecting a child, John the Baptist, and at her approach Elizabeth and John were filled with the Holy Spirit. We too must bring Christ to others as we help them in their needs, and by so doing we may be the occasion for the Spirit to come. At the beginning of Jesus' ministry, when He performed His first sign, Mary told the servants, 'Do whatever He tells you';[2] then, at its close, she stood by His cross (John 2:5 and 19:25). Her discipleship did not end with Jesus' infancy, and ours, too, must involve a sharing in Christ's Passion. Before Pentecost, Mary was present with the other disciples, a model of the Church praying for the continued coming of the Holy Spirit.

All Christ's disciples are redeemed by Christ. But the Church came to see that Mary is redeemed in a specially powerful way. We are set free from sin after it has had some hold on us; Mary was kept free from the sin that would otherwise have had a hold on her as a daughter of Adam. The doctrine of the *Immaculate Conception* teaches that Mary was conceived without stain of sin. That is, because of what her Son would do, and to fit her for her role, she was conceived with the life of grace already in her, and never subject to the warping of sin. This means that she is a sign of grace. Before she could do anything, she received God's gifts, and it was in the strength of those gifts that she was able to be obedient, and indeed to be without sin for the whole of her life. We all rely on God's gifts going before us; Mary did so most dramatically.

A recurring theme in theology is to draw a parallel between Mary and the Church, for as the model disciple, she is naturally the model of the Church. Mary is Mother of Christ, the Church is Mother of Christ. Since the Church is also the body of Christ, Mary His Mother can be seen as the *Mother of the Church* as well as her pre-eminent member. We glimpse this aspect of Mary's role when we read how Jesus, hanging on the cross, entrusted Mary and 'the disciple He loved' to each other as mother and son. Mary's maternal role is exercised by her specially powerful prayers, which help us 'come to birth' as Christ's members. At the close of her life Mary became the model of the Church in a specially encouraging way. The remains of the Apostles and early martyrs were cherished by the early Christians; but nowhere claims to preserve the body of Mary, for it is not in this world, it is already in heavenly glory. She already shares in the Resurrection of Jesus, as we hope to do. This is the doctrine of the *Assumption*, the taking up into glory of Mary's body. In her the saving work of Christ is completed; our hope is to 'catch up with her', and she helps us by her prayers as we imitate her pilgrimage of faith.

THE SACRAMENT OF THE KINGDOM

'The Church, in Christ, is like a sacrament – a sign and instrument, that is, of communion with God and of unity among all men' . . . In her, this unity is already begun, since she gathers men 'from every nation, from all tribes and peoples and tongues' [Apocalypse 7:9]; at the same time, the Church is the 'sign and instrument' of the full realization of the unity yet to come . . . [She] 'is the visible plan of God's love for humanity' . . .

(*Catechism* 775–776, quoting Vatican II,
Dogmatic Constitution on the Church, 1, and Paul VI,
discourse of 22 June 1973).

The Catholic Church is built up by the sacraments she celebrates; she is also herself a sacrament. In the sacraments God shows us what He is doing, and does what He shows us, in an outstanding way, which is not to say His work is confined to those occasions. In the Church, God shows us what He is doing, and does what He shows us, in the clearest if not the only way. What He is doing is bringing creation to its glorious fulfilment in His Kingdom; this work is begun now as sin is overcome by God's gentle love – which may sometimes be experienced with pain – and wholeness is restored, and the work is completed in the final resurrection. In Mary, and in the saints and others who have been specially open to God's grace, we see evil overcome and peace made. We have a glimpse of how we are to be filled with the Spirit of love and joy in the Kingdom.

Many people in the Church are not fully open to God's grace; she is a home for sinners as well as for saints, and the spotless Bride of Christ is disfigured by failures and hypocrisy. The fact that we do not all practise what we preach is no reason for despising the message of the Church – in fact, what we preach most of all is not moral rules but Christ Himself, who can heal our sinfulness, and those of us who preach are saying not 'Live as I live' but 'Come with me to Christ, and let Him help you live as He lived'. The members of the Church must try not to give scandal; but to take scandal is to refuse good food just because it is served up on a chipped plate.

We can draw a parallel between the Church and the Holy Eucharist. The Eucharist shows us Christ's work by the rite He gave us, and He is present in the Sacrament. We should approach Him there, regardless of the fact that some who approach Him are not prepared to derive much benefit from receiving Him. The Church shows us Christ's work by being the company of disciples He founded and by cherishing the hope He gave us; and He is present in her as His body. We should be joined to Him there, regardless of the fact that some of His disciples do not follow Him wholeheartedly. It is in the continuity of her historical identity, in her visible unity, in her infallible teaching of the faith, in her liturgy and especially in the sacraments, that the Church is herself sacramental. She points us back to the time when Jesus began to gather disciples round Himself. She shows us His reconciling work by being a structure that enables sinners and saints to proclaim their Christian faith, hope and love. She points us forward to the Kingdom in which sin and death will be overcome, and all of mankind that shall be saved will experience the unity and joy of the Blessed Trinity.

NOTES

1 Mortal sin by itself does not stop us being members of God's people; those who have faith but not charity are 'dead members' of the body of Christ and can be brought to life again in Him. It is apostasy and final impenitence that sever us from membership of Christ, the first being curable by grace.
2 That is basically her message at Lourdes and at the other places where Mary can reasonably be held to have appeared in recent decades.

SUGGESTIONS FOR READING

Convenient one-volume commentaries on the Bible
The Collegeville Bible Commentary (The Liturgical Press, Collegeville, MN, 1989/1992).
The New Jerome Biblical Commentary (Geoffrey Chapman, 1989).

Collections of official documents
The Christian Faith in the Doctrinal Documents of the Catholic Church, edited by J. Neuner and J. Dupuis (5th edition, HarperCollins, 1992). (This arranges documents – of varying authority – according to subject, and chronologically within each subject. Look at the heading of the document you are reading; usually it will state what the Church believes, but now and then it will be a list of *condemned* propositions!)
Vatican Council II: The Conciliar and Post-conciliar Documents; and *Vatican Council II: More Post-conciliar Documents*, edited by Austin Flannery (new edition, Dominican Publications, Dublin, 1992).

On the Creed
Jean-Noël Bezançon, Philippe Ferlay and Jean-Marie Onfray, *How to Understand the Creed* (SCM, 1987).

On the Fathers of the Church
J. N. D. Kelly, *Early Christian Doctrines* (5th edition, A. & C. Black, 1977).
A. Hamman, *How to Read the Church Fathers* (SCM, 1993)
The Faith of the Early Fathers, selected and translated by W. A. Jurgens (3 vols, The Liturgical Press, Collegeville, MN, 1970/1979). (This contains biographical and other notes. It includes, for information, writings of a few figures whose teachings were rejected by the Church.)

On St Thomas Aquinas
Josef Pieper, *Guide to Thomas Aquinas* (Notre Dame Press, 1962/1987).

Brian Davies, *The Thought of Thomas Aquinas* (Clarendon Press, Oxford, 1992).

Catechisms
A Catechism of Christian Doctrine (Catholic Truth Society, 1985).
Herbert McCabe, *The Teaching of the Catholic Church: A New Catechism of Christian Doctrine* (Catholic Truth Society, 1985).
Credo: A Catholic Catechism, compiled by the German Catechetical Association (Geoffrey Chapman, 1983/1984/Ignatius Press, USA).
Catechism of the Catholic Church, prepared at the request of the 1985 Synod of Bishops, approved by Pope John Paul II in 1992 (Geoffrey Chapman, 1994).

Introductions to the Catholic faith
Roderick Strange, *The Catholic Faith* (OUP, 1986).
James J. Killgallon, Mary Michael O'Shaughnessy OP and Gerard P. Weber, *Becoming Catholic Even If You Happen to Be One* (ACTA Foundation, Chicago/Geoffrey Chapman, 1980).

On Catholic theology and practice
Aidan Nichols, *The Shape of Catholic Theology* (T. & T. Clark, 1991). (A very thorough and balanced introduction to the sources and methods, and some of the issues, of Catholic theology.)
Philippe Béguerie and Claude Duchesneau, *How to Understand the Sacraments* (SCM, 1991).
Gerald O'Collins, *Interpreting Jesus* (Introducing Catholic Theology series; Geoffrey Chapman, 1983).
The New Dictionary of Theology, edited by Joseph A. Komonchak, Mary Collins and Dermot A. Lane (Gill & Macmillan, Dublin, 1987/1990).

INDEX

Adam, Adam and Eve 91–3, 126, 132–3, 173, 184, 187, 193
angels 20–3, 73, 88, 95
Anointing of the Sick 159, 181–3, 188
Apollinarius 112, 115
Apostles 165, 167–70, 185–6, 189, 194
Aristotle 14
Arius 37, 39, 112
Ascension of Jesus 125, 165
Assumption of Mary 194
Athanasius 37, 40, 46
Augustine 2–4, 15, 39–41, 48–9, 52, 74, 143, 146, 156, 184
authority, teaching, in the Church 6–7, 78, 82, 122, 186, 189–91
Baptism 2, 6, 8n, 34–5, 93, 124, 126, 158, 161–6, 169, 174, 176n, 177–8, 187
Baptism of Jesus 39, 54, 161–3, 166–7
Beatific Vision, blessedness, communion with God 26, 28–9, 39, 56–62, 71, 91, 122, 134, 151, 156
Benediction 154
Bible, Scriptures 2–8, 14–15, 20–2, 26, 29, 32, 43, 61, 73–4, 78, 82, 98, 101, 105, 124, 137, 140–9, 159–60, 173, 185–6, 190
See also Old Testament; New Testament; Gospels
bishops 7, 162, 165–72, 181–2, 186, 189–91
blasphemy against the Holy Spirit 99
body, human; risen 11, 23–5, 60–1
burial of the dead 60
celibacy 171–2, 191
Chalcedon 115–16
character, sacramental seal 163–6, 169
charismatic gifts 79
charity, *agapē* 71–80, 92, 94–6, 99–100, 120–1, 146, 164, 168, 192, 195
children of God viii, 2, 41, 59, 63, 69, 72–3, 79, 81, 85, 87, 90, 105, 109, 112, 137, 161–4, 179
Christian denominations/divisions/reunion 52–3, 143, 163, 186–8
church (as building) 142
Church, theology of 8n, 41, 62, 74, 89, 122, 126, 137, 142, 146, 148, 154–6, 161–4, 168–70, 174, 184–95
Church, (Roman) Catholic, as organization 2, 4–7, 44, 52, 74, 78, 146, 163, 170–2, 184–90, 194–5
City of God 62, 95, 184–5
conception 25–6
conception and birth of Jesus 32, 38, 114, 117–18
concupiscence 94
Confession 177–80, 188
Confirmation 159, 165–7, 170, 178
conscience 80, 82, 97, 134
consensus of the faithful/of theologians 7, 191

contemplation 140, 148–9, 191, 193
Council 6, 9n, 53, 190
See also specific Councils
courage, fortitude 80, 83–4
covenant 134, 141, 146, 158, 172–4
creation; createdness; dependence on God 13–22, 70–1, 141, 158–9, 161
Creed 5–6, 34, 52, 74, 117, 146
Cyril of Alexandria 113–15
Dante 42
deacons 162, 168–71
death 89, 94, 101–7, 128, 131, 135, 182, 192, 195
definition/development of doctrine 6–7, 190
Descent into Hell 132–3
divinization 40, 56, 58, 69–71, 116, 123, 163
See also grace; Trinity, sharing the relationships of
Easter Sunday/Vigil 92, 125, 142, 154, 163, 165
Eastern/Western Churches/Rite 52–3, 139–40, 166–7, 171–4, 186–7
emotions, drives 25, 28, 83–4, 94
Ephesus 114
equity 85, 98
eternal life 56, 58, 101
Eucharist/Holy Communion/Mass 6, 19, 22, 33, 42, 80, 126, 135, 139–43, 146–8, 150–9, 163–5, 169–72, 174, 178–9, 181–2, 184, 188, 195
as Sacrifice 154–8, 169, 181
Eutyches 114
evil 2–3, 67, 87–91, 124
experience, religious/mystical 70–1
faith 1–4, 71–4, 77–8, 98, 146, 159, 164, 166, 184–5, 195
and reason vii, 14, 74, 116
implicit 159, 185
Fall 91–5, 177
fasting and abstinence 80, 107, 156, 180
Father, God the; Abba 2, 34–42, 46–55, 58–9, 63, 67–71, 77–80, 106, 109, 112, 117–31, 137, 146–8, 156, 193
flesh (in pejorative sense) 94–5, 100
Florence, Council of 53
forgiveness 30–2, 71, 101–3, 125, 130–2, 177–81
freedom/free will 3, 16, 20, 26, 28, 64, 77–9, 85, 90–1, 94–6, 104–5, 131–5
friendship of/with God vii, 31, 56–8, 64, 76–8, 87, 97–8, 100, 106, 119, 166, 177–8, 184, 192
glorification 28, 59–64, 87, 134, 151, 156, 167, 183
God 1, 3, 11–20, 29–32, and *passim*
changeless, not complex, eternal, one 14–15, 20, 30, 34–41, 49, 58, 88, 92, 114

198

Index 199